ST(P) MATHEMATICS 3
Teacher's Notes and Aı

ST(P) MATHEMATICS series:

ST(P) 1A
ST(P) 1B
ST(P) 1A Teacher's Notes and Answers
ST(P) 1B Teacher's Notes and Answers

ST(P) 2A
ST(P) 2B
ST(P) 2A Teacher's Notes and Answers
ST(P) 2B Teacher's Notes and Answers

ST(P) 3A
ST(P) 3B
ST(P) 3A Teacher's Notes and Answers
ST(P) 3B Teacher's Notes and Answers

ST(P) 4A
ST(P) 4B
ST(P) 4A Teacher's Notes and Answers
ST(P) 4B Teacher's Notes and Answers

ST(P) 5A (with answers)
ST(P) 5B (with answers)

ST(P) 5C
ST(P) 5C Copy Masters
ST(P) 5C Teacher's Notes and Answers

ST(P) Resource Book

ST(P) Workbooks:
Drawing and Using Curved Graphs
Measuring Instruments
Symmetry and Transformation
Straight Line Graphs

ST(P) MATHEMATICS 3B

Teacher's Notes and Answers

L. Bostock, B.Sc.

S. Chandler, B.Sc.

A. Shepherd, B.Sc.

E. Smith, M.Sc.

Stanley Thornes (Publishers) Ltd

First published in 1986 by:
Stanley Thornes (Publishers) Ltd
Old Station Drive
Leckhampton
CHELTENHAM GL53 0DN
England

Second edition 1991

British Library Cataloguing in Publication Data
ST(P) mathematics 3B. 2nd ed.
   Teacher's notes and answers.
   1. Mathematics
   I. Bostock, L.
   510

ISBN 0-7487-0545-7

Typeset by Tech-Set, Gateshead, Tyne & Wear.
Printed and bound in Great Britain by
Ebenezer Baylis and Son Ltd, The Trinity Press, Worcester, and London.

CONTENTS

INTRODUCTION

This book is part of the ST(P) graded series in mathematics and is intended for use in the third year of secondary schools. It should enable pupils to reach about Level 6 of the National Curriculum in mathematics for Key Stage 3, but we have tried to make the contents of this book as flexible as possible to allow teachers to plot their own courses through it. Hence many of the topics that appear in Books 1B and 2B are also included here; these sections can be used for further consolidation with the lower ability pupils or they can be used sparingly as quick reminders when necessary with the more able pupils.

Some of the work in this book goes beyond Level 6; this is in preparation for Key Stage 4 at the age of 16 plus. Some teachers may decide that topics mentioned in Level 7, such as Pythagoras' Theorem and flow charts, can be left until the fourth year. Books 4B and 5B continue to develop the mathematics necessary for intermediate level at GCSE.

Pupils need calculators with brackets and memory functions and it is desirable that they also have a $\boxed{\pi}$ button and squaring facilities; this probably means that they will have to own a simple scientific calculator. We have indicated in the text that squaring can be done by using the $\boxed{x^2}$ button; on some calculators this needs two key strokes, e.g. $\boxed{\text{INV}}$ $\boxed{\sqrt{}}$. Although it is desirable that simple calculations should be done without a calculator, there are a few pupils who never grasp the basic number work and such pupils should be allowed to use their calculators freely.

As is the case with the earlier books in this series, there is a plentiful supply of carefully graded exercises. Questions that have a single underline, e.g. **12.**, are extra, but not harder, questions for further practice or for later revision. Harder questions have a double underline, e.g. **12.**, and, for the less able pupils, should be used only for discussion. We have introduced multiple choice questions in this book. These can be useful teaching aids when used for discussion: they are often a better test of understanding than straightforward exercises.

In this answer book we have included some mental tests which are graded to correspond to the order of work in the text book. We have also included some copymasters for use at appropriate places in the text, and the notes that follow indicate where these are needed. There are also references to additional copymasters which are to be found in *ST(P) Mathematics Resource Book* and in *ST(P) Mathematics 5C Copymasters*.

The text is brief and aims to supply explanations for those who wish to remind themselves of the reasons for what they are doing, although in most cases it does not supply a complete introduction to a new topic.

You will notice that the decimal point has been lowered in this book to conform with the general convention of mathematical and scientific typesetting.

NOTES AND ANSWERS

CHAPTER 1   Number Work

The work in this chapter is mainly revision. New work is included in some sections and this is indicated at the start of the answers to the relevant exercise.

EXERCISE 1a
(p. 1)

1. 500
2. 7000, 7
3. $400 - 40 = 360$
4. 1000
5. 303
6. 222, 225, 252, 255, 522, 525, 552, 555
7. a) four thousand, seven hundred and eighty-two
   b) one million
8. a) 203   b) 1078
9. a) 6   b) 60   c) 62
10. a) 8   b) 18   c) 80
11. a) one hundred and twenty-seven
    b) three thousand, seven hundred and eighty-nine

EXERCISE 1b
(p. 2)

1. 2, 3, 5, 7
2. 2, 3, 5, 7, 11
3. 13, 17, 19
4. 2, 3, 5, 7
5. 5, 7, 11, 13
6. 23
7. no

EXERCISE 1c
(p. 3)

1. a) yes   b) no   c) yes   d) no   e) yes
2. last figure is even
3. a) no   b) yes   c) yes   d) no   e) yes
4. last figure is 0 or 5
5. a) 8, 16, 40, 206   b) 40, 35, 515
6. a) yes   b) yes   c) no   d) yes   e) no
7. 6, yes
8. a) 12, yes   b) 3, yes

EXERCISE 1d
(p. 4)

1. 1, 2, 3, 6
2. 1, 2, 4, 8
3. 1, 2, 5, 10
4. 1, 2, 4
5. 1, 3, 9
6. 1, 2, 3, 6, 9, 18
7. 1, 3, 5, 15
8. 1, 19
9. 1, 3, 7, 21
10. 1, 2, 13, 26
11. 1, 3, 17, 21 5)
12. 1, 2, 4, 8, 16

13. a) 1, 2, 3, 4, 8, 12, 24   b) 2, 3

1

EXERCISE 1e
(p. 5)

1. 2×5
2. 3×7
3. 5×7
4. $2 \times 2 \times 3$

5. $2 \times 2 \times 2$
6. $2 \times 2 \times 7$
7. $2 \times 2 \times 3 \times 5$
8. $2 \times 5 \times 5$

9. $2 \times 2 \times 3 \times 3$
10. $2 \times 3 \times 11$
11. $2 \times 3 \times 3 \times 7$
12. $2 \times 2 \times 3 \times 3 \times 3$

EXERCISE 1f
(p. 5)

1. a) 2, 6, 8, 10, 12, 14, 16, 18, 20
   b) 3, 6, 12, 15, 18
   c) 8, 12, 16, 20
   d) 5, 10, 15, 20
   e) 6, 12, 18
   f) 8, 16
2. a) 7, 14, 21, 28
   b) 5, 10, 15, 20
   c) 8, 16, 24, 32
   d) 10, 20, 30, 40
   e) 12, 24, 36, 48
   f) 15, 30, 45, 60

3. 54, 63, 72, 81, 90, 99
4. 14, 21, 28, 35, 42, 49

EXERCISE 1g
(p. 6)

1. 4, 9
2. 16, 25, 36, 49, 64, 81, 100

3. 4, 16
4. 4, 16, 64

EXERCISE 1h
(p. 6)

Encourage pupils to think of the easiest way of dealing with multiplication: $2 \times 8 \times 9 \times 5 = 10 \times 72$ rather than $16 \times 9 \times 5$ etc.

1. 24
2. 30
3. 40
4. 28

5. 60
6. 96
7. 105
8. 120

9. 30
10. 60
11. 36
12. 42

EXERCISE 1i
(p. 7)

1. 4
2. 27
3. 16
4. 16

5. 25
6. 64
7. 125
8. 81

9. 49
10. 8
11. 256
12. 216

13. a) 32   b) 9   c) 288
14. 108

EXERCISE 1j
(p. 8)

A possible mistake is mentally to insert brackets in the wrong place in the calculation of $8 - 2 + 6$ and say it is $8 - 8$

1. 4
2. 6
3. 11

4. 7
5. 5
6. 16

7. 4
8. 13
9. 9

10. 18
11. 20
12. 20

13. 1
14. 10
15. 4

16. 2
17. 3
18. 27

19. 11	**22.** 5	**25.** 4
20. 20	**23.** 0	**26.** 10
21. 5	**24.** 4	**27.** 30

EXERCISE 1k (New work)
(p. 8)

1. $1\frac{1}{2}$	**4.** $2\frac{1}{2}$	**7.** 8
2. 2	**5.** 2	**8.** 4
3. $3\frac{1}{2}$	**6.** $\frac{1}{4}$	**9.** $\frac{6}{9}$ or $\frac{2}{3}$

EXERCISE 1l   **1.**   a) 4   b) -2 c) 3
(p. 9)

2. 5	**6.** 11	**10.** -1
3. 4	**7.** 2	**11.** 7
4. -5	**8.** 0	**12.** -1
5. -6	**9.** -2	**13.** -11

14. -8	**17.** -4	**20.** -3
15. -9	**18.** -7	**21.** -2
16. 3	**19.** -6	**22.** -6

EXERCISE 1m
(p. 10)

1. 1.5	**6.** 14	**11.** 9
2. 21	**7.** 2.3	**12.** 2.5
3. 15	**8.** 6.5	**13.** 5
4. 3.5	**9.** 6	**14.** 6.5
5. 5	**10.** 0.5	**15.** 8.5

EXERCISE 1n (New work)
(p. 11)

1. 81 000	**3.** 120 000	**5.** 40 000
2. 22 000	**4.** 49 000	**6.** 96 000

7. 70	**9.** 60	**11.** 1200
8. 12	**10.** 12	**12.** 120

13. 1200	**17.** 200
14. 20 000	**18.** 200
15. 30	**19.** 5
16. 12 000 cm or 120 m	**20.** 16 000

EXERCISE 1p
(p. 13)

1. 1610	**4.** 8820	**7.** 6665
2. 1326	**5.** 2829	**8.** 1178
3. 3216	**6.** 5162	**9.** 12 688

10. 1008	**15.** £756
11. a) 2678 b) 6592	**16.** 969 minutes
12. 389	**17.** a) 7200 p b) £72
13. £19.68	**18.** a) £66.24 b) £18.24
14. 3458	

EXERCISE 1q
(p. 14)

1. 15, rem 5
2. 18, rem 2
3. 24, rem 1

4. 24, rem 1
5. 13, rem 7
6. 14, rem 2

7. 22, rem 7
8. 15, rem 5
9. 62

10. 64, rem 2
11. 13
12. 101

13. 18, rem 2
14. 26
15. 68, rem 1

16. 12, rem 3
17. 30, rem 1
18. 20, rem 1

19. 13, 4
20. 27
21. 28, 4

22. £36 each, £3 to charity
23. 192, 6 over

EXERCISE 1r
(p. 15)

1. 12
2. 24
3. 36

4. 32
5. 22
6. 18

7. 19
8. 29
9. 19

10. 27
11. 12

12. 26
13. 21

14. 45
15. 34

16. 17
17. 14 hours
18. 72 inches

19. a) 420 mm   b) 30
20. a) 58   b) 4 cm

EXERCISE 1s
(p. 16)

1. a) 2, 5, 41   b) 1, 5, 9, 21, 39, 41   c) 2, 12, 18, 36
   d) 2, 12, 18, 36   e) 9, 12, 18, 21, 36, 39   f) 1, 2, 9, 12, 18, 36
2. a) 2   b) 5   c) 4
3. a) 6   b) 20   c) 6
4. a) 11   b) 14   c) 14
5. a) 1035   b) 9, rem 3

EXERCISE 1t
(p. 17)

1. a) 5, 15, 21, 23, 27, 29   b) 5, 15, 20   c) 4, 5, 8, 20
   d) 5, 23, 29   e) 4, 6, 8, 12, 20   f) 4, 8, 12, 20
2. a) 128   b) 28   c) 8
3. 19, rem 1
4. a) 3808   b) 23
5. $3000 - 4 = 2996$

EXERCISE 1u
(p. 17)

1. C   2. D   3. A   4. A   5. B

CHAPTER 2   Patterns and Sequences

EXERCISE 2a
(p. 18)

Most pupils will enjoy drawing and continuing these patterns but care should be taken not to spend too much time at it. There is a copymaster for questions 1 to 6 at the end of this book and they can be supplemented by copymaster 44 from *ST(P) Mathematics 5C Copymasters*.

EXERCISE 2b
(p. 20)

A supply of squared paper is required for this exercise.

1.
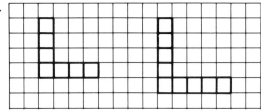

2.
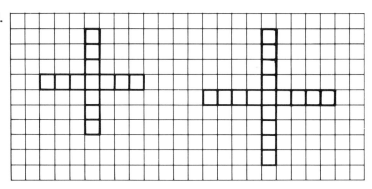

3.
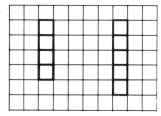

4.
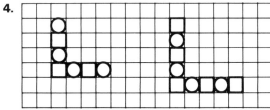

5.
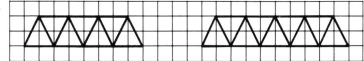

6.

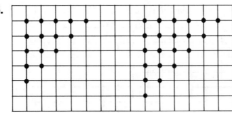

7.

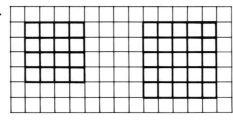

8.

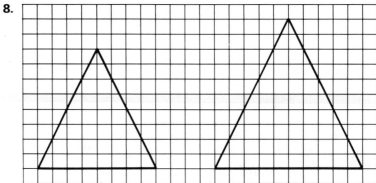

9.

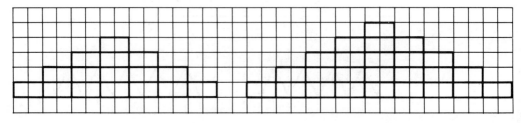

10.

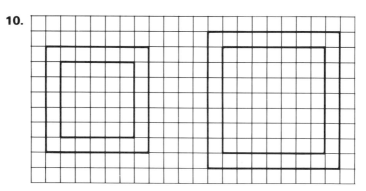

EXERCISE 2c
(p. 22)

1. 2, 5, 8, 11, 14,
2. 5, 10, 15, 20, 25,
3. 1, 2, 3, 5, 8,
4. 50, 47, 44, 41, 38,

5. 100, 90, 80, 70, 60,
6. 3, 6, 12, 24, 48,
7. 1, 3, 9, 27, 81,
8. 20, 18, 16, 14, 12,

9. 15, 18,
10. 21, 25,
11. 64, 128,

12. 23, 30
13. 4, 2,
14. 14, 19,

15. add 5, 24, 29,
16. add 5, 23, 28,

17. double it, 80, 160,
18. subtract 4, 44, 40,

EXERCISE 2d
(p. 23)

1. 1, 4, 9, 16, 25, 36, 49, 64,
2. 1, 3, 6, 10, 15, 21, 28, 36,
3. all the numbers, except 5, are rectangular numbers

6 • • •
  • • •

12 • • • •   • • • • •
   • • • •   • • • • • •
   • • • •

15 • • • • •
   • • • • •
   • • • • •

16 • • • •   • • • • • • • •
   • • • •   • • • • • • • •
   • • • •
   • • • •

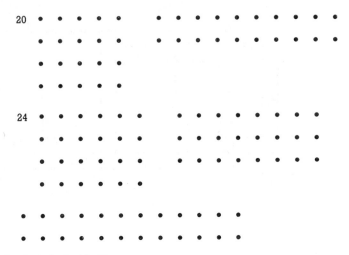

4. 4, 6, 8, 9, 10, 12,

5. 11, 13, 17, they are all prime numbers

6. a)

	1st		2nd		3rd		4th		5th		6th		7th		8th
Square numbers	1		4		9		16		25		36		49		64
First differences		3		5		7		9		11		13		15	
Second differences			2		2		2		2		2		2		2

b) yes – add 2 each time

c) yes – add 0 each time

7. a) 16, 32, 64, 128,

b)

	1st		2nd		3rd		4th		5th		6th		7th		8th
Sequence	1		2		4		8		16		32		64		128
First differences		1		2		4		8		16		32		64	
Second differences			1		2		4		8		16		32		

c) yes – they give the original sequence

d) yes – they give the original sequence

8. a) The first eight triangular numbers are   1, 3, 6, 10, 15, 21, 28, 36,

b)

	1st		2nd		3rd		4th		5th		6th		7th		8th
Sequence	1		3		6		10		15		21		28		36
First differences		2		3		4		5		6		7		8	
Second differences			1		1		1		1		1		1		1

c) yes – add 1 each time

d) yes – add 0 each time

9. a)

Diagram number	1	2	3	4
Number of squares	1	5	9	13

b) 17, 21

d) four

10. a)

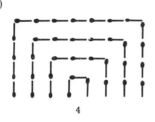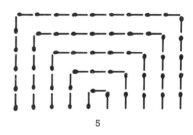

4   5

b) 3, 10, 21, 36, 55,

c)

Diagram number	1	2	3	4	5
Number of matchsticks	3	10	21	36	55

d) 78

11. a)

	9		32		75		144		245		384	
First difference		23		43		69		101		139		
Second difference			20		26		32		38		44	
Third difference				6		6		6		6		6

b) yes – each number is 6

c) 44 (38 + 6), 50 (44 + 6)

d) 183 (139 + 44), 233 (183 + 50)

e) 567 (384 + 183), 800 (567 + 233)

12. a)

	6		24		60		120		210		336	
Sequence	6		24		60		120		210		336	
First differences		18		36		60		90		126		168
Second differences			18		24		30		36		42	
Third differences				6		6		6		6		6

b) yes – each number is 6

c) 42 (36 + 6), 48 (42 + 6)

d) 168 (126 + 42), 216 (168 + 48)

e) 504 (336 + 168), 720 (504 + 216)

CHAPTER 3   Fractions and Decimals ▬▬▬▬▬▬▬▬▬

Much of the work in this chapter is revision but there is some new work. Those exercises that are purely revision of work in 1B and 2B are indicated: these can be used sparingly for those pupils that have thoroughly grasped the ideas.

EXERCISE 3a   Revises the meaning of fractions.
(p. 27)

1. $\frac{1}{2}$ **3.** $\frac{5}{8}$ **5.** $\frac{1}{2}$ **7.** $\frac{5}{6}$ **9.** $\frac{1}{2}$

2. $\frac{2}{5}$ **4.** $\frac{8}{15}$ **6.** $\frac{5}{6}$ **8.** $\frac{5}{9}$ **10.** $\frac{3}{5}$

11. $\frac{8}{12}$

12. $\frac{5}{15}$

13. a) 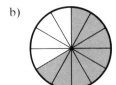   b)

Copymaster 4 in the resource book can be used for these circles.

EXERCISE 3b   Revision of the basic method but using a wider range of fractions.
(p. 29)   Calculators can be used.

1. £16   **5.** £15   **9.** £30
2. £12   **6.** 42 m   **10.** 140 cm
3. 63 cm   **7.** £536   **11.** £96
4. 45 kg   **8.** 288 g   **12.** 265 kg

13. a) 8 m   b) 28 m
14. a) £108   b) £864   c) £108
15. a) 36   b) $\frac{1}{6}$ c) overestimated by three stone

EXERCISE 3c   This is revision but using a larger range of fractions.
(p. 31)

1. $\frac{1}{4} = \frac{②}{8}$ **5.** $\frac{2}{5} = \frac{④}{10}$ **9.** $\frac{5}{9} = \frac{⑮}{27}$

2. $\frac{3}{4} = \frac{⑨}{12}$ **6.** $\frac{1}{3} = \frac{③}{9}$ **10.** $\frac{3}{8} = \frac{⑫}{32}$

3. $\frac{1}{8} = \frac{2}{⑯}$ **7.** $\frac{3}{5} = \frac{9}{⑮}$ **11.** $\frac{2}{3} = \frac{6}{9}$

4. $\frac{2}{3} = \frac{8}{⑫}$ **8.** $\frac{3}{7} = \frac{6}{⑭}$ **12.** $\frac{3}{4} = \frac{12}{16}$

13. $\dfrac{3}{10} = \dfrac{9}{30}$ **15.** $\dfrac{4}{5} = \dfrac{16}{20}$ **17.** e.g. $\dfrac{4}{10}, \dfrac{6}{15}, \dfrac{20}{50}$

14. $\dfrac{1}{12} = \dfrac{3}{36}$ **16.** $\dfrac{5}{8} = \dfrac{15}{24}$ **18.** e.g. $\dfrac{2}{4}, \dfrac{3}{6}, \dfrac{100}{200}$

EXERCISE 3d This is revision.
(p. 32)

1. $\frac{2}{3}$ **5.** $\frac{1}{2}$ **9.** $\frac{2}{3}$ **13.** $\frac{4}{5}$

2. $\frac{1}{2}$ **6.** $\frac{1}{3}$ **10.** $\frac{3}{4}$ **14.** $\frac{3}{5}$

3. $\frac{1}{5}$ **7.** $\frac{1}{4}$ **11.** $\frac{1}{4}$ **15.** $\frac{5}{9}$

4. $\frac{1}{3}$ **8.** $\frac{3}{4}$ **12.** $\frac{3}{4}$ **16.** $\frac{2}{3}$

EXERCISE 3e This is new work and concentrates mainly on addition and subtraction of
(p. 33) fractions with equal denominators. Questions 25 to 28 are intended as an
introduction to adding fractions with different denominators; this can be
extended by asking pupils to add two fractions without giving them a
diagram (they have to devise their own). From this some pupils may be
able to deduce a general rule for adding fractions.

1. $\frac{4}{5}$ **4.** $\frac{4}{9}$ **7.** $\frac{11}{13}$

2. $\frac{3}{7}$ **5.** $\frac{2}{5}$ **8.** $\frac{3}{10}$

3. $\frac{1}{11}$ **6.** $\frac{4}{5}$ **9.** $\frac{7}{9}$

10. $\frac{1}{2}$ **15.** $\frac{1}{5}$ **20.** $\frac{1}{4}$

11. $\frac{1}{5}$ **16.** $\frac{1}{3}$ **21.** 1

12. $\frac{3}{10}$ **17.** $\frac{1}{2}$ **22.** $\frac{1}{4}$

13. $\frac{1}{2}$ **18.** 1   **23.** $\frac{1}{6}$

14. $\frac{1}{3}$ **19.** 1   **24.** 1

25. a) $\frac{1}{2}$ b) $\frac{1}{12}$ c) $\frac{7}{12}$ d) $\frac{7}{12}$

26. a) $\frac{1}{2}$ b) $\frac{1}{6}$ c) $\frac{2}{3}$

27. c) $\frac{1}{2}$

28. a) $\frac{7}{12}$ b) $\frac{31}{36}$ c) $\frac{11}{18}$

EXERCISE 3f **1.** $2\frac{1}{2}$ **4.** $1\frac{3}{4}$ **7.** $1\frac{2}{3}$ **10.** $2\frac{1}{5}$
(p. 36)
2. $1\frac{1}{3}$ **5.** $1\frac{4}{5}$ **8.** $3\frac{1}{2}$ **11.** $1\frac{1}{8}$

3. $2\frac{1}{3}$ **6.** $2\frac{1}{7}$ **9.** $2\frac{1}{4}$ **12.** $5\frac{2}{3}$

13. $\frac{5}{3}$ **16.** $\frac{7}{5}$ **19.** $\frac{4}{3}$ **22.** $\frac{23}{7}$

14. $\frac{5}{2}$ **17.** $\frac{10}{3}$ **20.** $\frac{11}{5}$ **23.** $\frac{17}{4}$

15. $\frac{7}{4}$ **18.** $\frac{9}{4}$ **21.** $\frac{5}{4}$ **24.** $\frac{15}{4}$

The rest of the work in this chapter revises the work on decimals in books 1B and 2B but in all cases extends it to include the third decimal place.

EXERCISE 3g (p. 37)

1. a) 3 tens   b) 3 hundredths   c) 3 units   d) 3 thousandths
   e) 3 tenths
2. a) 6.19   b) 2.009
3. 20, 2.8, 0.22, 0.022
4. 4
5. 1.7
6. 1.07
7. 4.57 and 4.570
8. 0.24
9. a) $\frac{1}{2}$ b) $\frac{1}{4}$ c) $\frac{1}{20}$ d) $\frac{1}{200}$

EXERCISE 3h (p. 38)

1. 1.9
2. 0.5
3. 4.4
4. 1.14
5. 0.728
6. 1.62
7. 1.3
8. 4.7
9. 1.03
10. 6.04
11. 5.17
12. 6.75
13. 27.8
14. 15.08
15. 14.4
16. 16.5
17. 0.27
18. 2.28

EXERCISE 3i (p. 39)

1. $\frac{1}{2}$
2. $\frac{1}{25}$
3. $\frac{4}{5}$
4. $\frac{3}{20}$
5. $\frac{3}{100}$
6. $1\frac{7}{20}$
7. $\frac{1}{8}$
8. $1\frac{1}{4}$
9. $\frac{1}{500}$
10. $\frac{1}{125}$
11. $\frac{3}{4}$
12. $3\frac{3}{4}$
13. $\frac{7}{10}$
14. $\frac{1}{20}$
15. $\frac{1}{4}$
16. $\frac{1}{200}$
17. 0.5
18. 0.25
19. 0.4
20. 0.7
21. 0.375
22. 0.03
23. 2.5
24. 1.25
25. 3.125
26. 1.75
27. 0.14
28. 0.625
29. 0.6
30. 0.12
31. 0.27
32. 2.75

	Fraction	Decimal
33.	$\frac{4}{5}$	0.8
34.	$\frac{1}{4}$	0.25
35.	$\frac{3}{4}$	0.75
36.	$\frac{1}{2}$	0.5
37.	$1\frac{9}{10}$	1.9
38.	$\frac{1}{8}$	0.125

39. a) 0.875   b) 1.3   c) 0.28

EXERCISE 3j **(p. 40)**	**1.** 48	**8.** 0.316	**15.** 520
	2. 0.48	**9.** 2.5	**16.** 0.17
	3. 3.4	**10.** 1005	**17.** 240
	4. 0.055	**11.** 73.1	**18.** 0.0002
	5. 1250	**12.** 52	**19.** 400
	6. 0.0974	**13.** 0.078	**20.** 0.552
	7. 87	**14.** 0.004	**21.** 3.2

EXERCISE 3k **(p. 41)**	**1.** 70.09	**6.** 29.76	**11.** 0.0486
	2. 2.6	**7.** 5.875	**12.** 8
	3. 1.296	**8.** 56.32	**13.** 10.725
	4. 0.4	**9.** 250	**14.** 1383.38
	5. 6.48	**10.** 250	**15.** 0.025

16. 750
17. $6.39 \, \text{m}^2$
18. 1800
19. 12 whole pieces
20. 65

EXERCISE 3l **(p. 43)**	**1.** 1.4	**3.** 0.2	**5.** 0.1	**7.** 2.4
	2. 2.8	**4.** 0.1	**6.** 5.0	**8.** 5.1

	9. 0.09	**11.** 0.13	**13.** 0.03	**15.** 52.37
	10. 2.04	**12.** 10.10	**14.** 0.01	**16.** 0.06

17. 8.127	**20.** 0.002	**23.** 0.001
18. 2.034	**21.** 0.024	**24.** 0.010
19. 4.667	**22.** 0.130	**25.** 1.028

26. 0.0127	**29.** 0.0005	**32.** 20.3051
27. 2.4699	**30.** 1.8321	**33.** 1.0080
28. 3.8003	**31.** 10.8826	**34.** 10.0000

35. 82.17	**38.** 0.0128	**41.** 27.294
36. 20.2	**39.** 1.361	**42.** 0.0069
37. 7.708	**40.** 15.8	**43.** 0.080

EXERCISE 3m
(p. 44)

1. £19.29
2. a) 350°   b) 205°   c) 275°
3. 66.9 m
4. a) £13.85   b) £2.94   c) £15.38
5. a) 224 cm   b) 177 cm   c) 57 cm
6. a) 51 g   b) 158 g   c) 2888 g
7. 2.6 kg to the nearest tenth of a kilogram (accept any reasonable answer, e.g. 2.5 kg, but an answer to 3 s.f. is not realistic for this problem). Apples vary in weight.

EXERCISE 3n
(p. 45)

1. a) 5.56   b) 4.835   c) 7.21   d) 0.412

2. a) $\frac{3}{4}$ b) $\frac{1}{25}$ c) $\frac{3}{20}$ d) $\frac{21}{200}$

3. a) 0.286   b) 0.067   c) 0.556   d) 0.667

4. 1.222 ($1\frac{2}{9}$), 1.58, 1.62, 1.714 ($1\frac{5}{7}$)

5. a) 0.4   b) £22.41

6. 9.92 m

7. £35.38

8. $1\frac{3}{7}$

9. c) $\frac{17}{24}$

10. £53.85

EXERCISE 3p
(p. 46)

1. $\frac{7}{5}$

2. $\frac{2}{3}$

3. 270

4. 1.5

5. 27 cm

6. 0.052

7. 0.023

8. $2\frac{5}{9}$

9. $\frac{8}{12}$

10. 0.38

EXERCISE 3q
(p. 46)

1. C   **3.** B   **5.** B

2. A   **4.** D   **6.** D

CHAPTER 4   Reflections and Rotations

A good supply of small pieces of tracing paper is required for this chapter. To avoid pupils marking the text book, the questions in those exercises can be copied on squared paper and duplicated for distribution. Copymasters 15–19 from 5C can be used for revision of line and rotational symmetry.

Copymasters 37, 38 and 45 from 5C give extra practice in reflections.

Copymasters 40–43 from 5C give extra practice in rotations.

EXERCISE 4a
(p. 48)

1.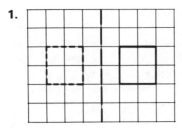

2.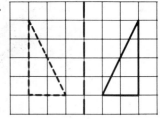

3.

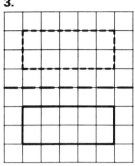

6.

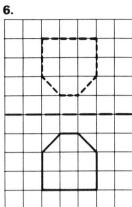

4.

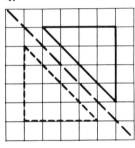

7.

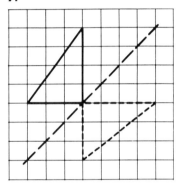

5.

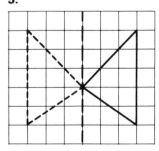

8.

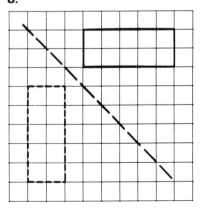

9.

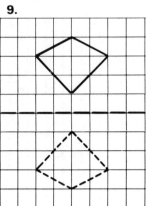

13.

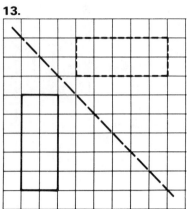

10.

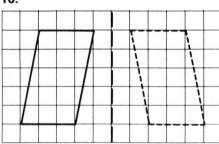

11.

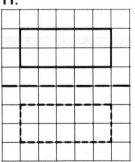

14.

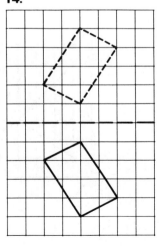

12.

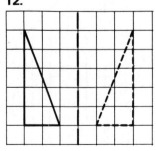

15.

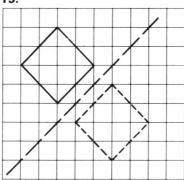

18.

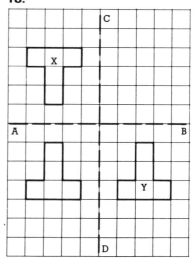

16.

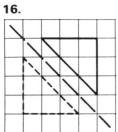

17.

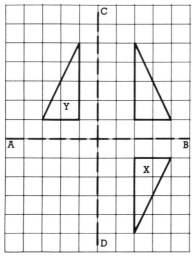

19.

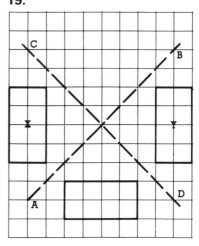

20.

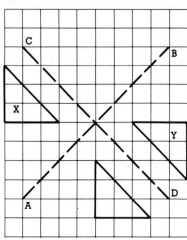

22.

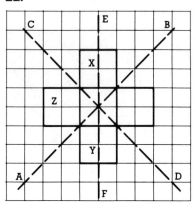

21.

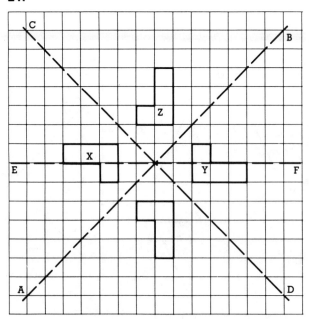

23.

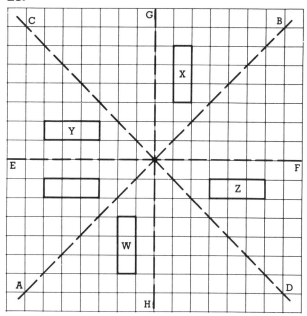

EXERCISE 4b   **1.** 2   **3.** 4   **5.** 2
(p. 54)   **2.** 3   **4.** 5   **6.** 3

EXERCISE 4c   **1.**   **2.**
(p. 57)

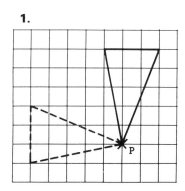

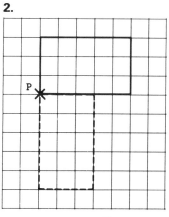

3.

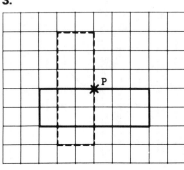

6.

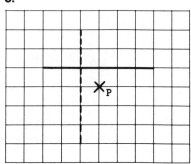

4.

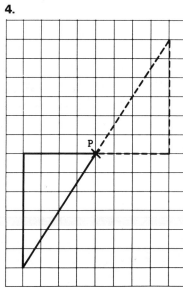

7.

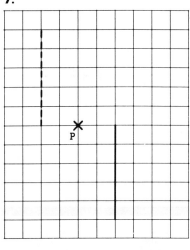

5.

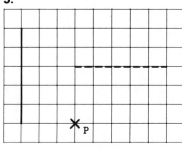

8.

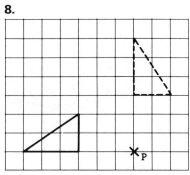

9.

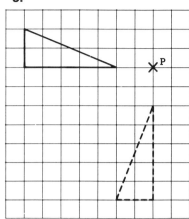

10.

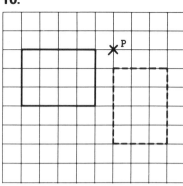

CHAPTER 5   Algebra

The first two exercises in this chapter revise and consolidate the solution of linear equations. The remainder of this chapter goes beyond Level 6 work. This is in preparation for Level 7/8, and, although we think it is desirable to start this work now, it can be postponed. For those pupils who will be attempting only the lowest level GCSE, it should be omitted.

EXERCISE 5a
(p. 59)

1. 4
2. 4
3. 2

4. 6
5. 13
6. 2

7. 4
8. 3
9. 10

10. Take 4 from each side, $x = 2$
11. Add 7 to each side, $x = 16$
12. Divide both sides by 3, $x = 2$
13. Divide both sides by 5, $c = 3$
14. Take 3 from each side, $y = 4$

15. Add 4 to each side, $z = 9$
16. Take 5 from each side, $z = 5$
17. Divide both sides by 3, $y = 5$
18. Add 9 to each side, $x = 11$

19. $x + 114 = 180$; angle is $66°$
20. $x + 280 = 360$; angle is $80°$

21. $x + 130 = 180$; angle is $50°$
22. $3x = 180$; angle is $60°$

EXERCISE 5b
(p. 60)

Abbreviations can be used when writing down what is being done to each side:

$$2x + 3 = 11$$
$$-3 \quad -3$$
$$2x = 8$$
$$\div 2 \quad \div 2$$
$$x = 4$$

It is better not to leave out the instructions altogether.

1. 3	**7.** 3	**13.** 1
2. 6	**8.** 9	**14.** 3
3. 4	**9.** 9	**15.** 9
4. 3	**10.** 1	**16.** 3
5. 5	**11.** 2.5	**17.** 3
6. 8	**12.** 1.5	**18.** 4

EXERCISE 5c
(p. 61)

1, 3, 4, 6 and **8** are expressions.
2. 4
5. 5
7. 3 (and −3)
9. 6

10. $4z$	**14.** $3a$	**18.** $6x$
11. $5y$	**15.** x^3	**19.** a^3
12. $5t$	**16.** $5y$	**20.** $4b$
13. s^2	**17.** $9b$	**21.** $2z$

EXERCISE 5d
(p. 62)

2, 4, 6 and **11** cannot be simplified.

1. $5x + 4$	**8.** $5x + y$	**13.** $3x + 3$
3. $x + 4$	**9.** $4a$	**14.** $2y + 6$
5. $10 - 2x$	**10.** $2c + 3d$	**15.** $5x + 3y$
7. $2z + 6$	**12.** $x + 2$	

16. $3x = 9; x = 3$	**20.** $3b = 3; b = 1$
17. $7y = 14; y = 2$	**21.** $6c = 18; c = 3$
18. $10a = 20; a = 2$	**22.** $4x = 4; x = 1$
19. $x = 10$	**23.** $3z = 24; z = 8$

24. 2	**28.** 3
25. 3	**29.** 2
26. 3	**30.** 3
27. 6	**31.** 2

32. $x + 2x + 100 + 110 = 360$; angle is 50°
33. $x + 3x + x = 160; x = 32$

EXERCISE 5e
(p. 64)

This work on negative numbers is needed to develop skills necessary to cope with the plotting of graphs later on in this book, and for coping with the solution of simultaneous equations.

1. $3x$	**6.** c	**11.** $-2y$
2. $-3y$	**7.** $-7x$	**12.** $-2x$
3. $-2a$	**8.** $-5y$	**13.** 0
4. p	**9.** $-3x$	**14.** $-2z$
5. $-2b$	**10.** $3a$	**15.** 0

EXERCISE 5f
(p. 65)

1. $6y$
2. ab
3. $5y$
4. $15x^2$
5. $14z$
6. $15t$
7. cd
8. $12s^2$
9. $5t^2$
10. $24h$
11. yz (or zy)
12. $6r^2$

13. $16x$
14. cannot be simplified
15. $1 + 3y$
16. $4s$
17. 2
18. cannot be simplified
19. $2pq$
20. $2p^2$
21. $11x$
22. cannot be simplified
23. $3x^2$
24. $3xy$
25. cannot be simplified
26. $6x$
27. cannot be simplified

EXERCISE 5g
(p. 66)

1. $2x + 10$
2. $5a - 20$
3. $7y + 7$
4. $3z + 6$
5. $8 + 4y$
6. $8 - 4y$
7. $6x + 12$
8. $12x - 20$
9. $9x + 18$
10. $6x - 18$
11. $25 + 10x$
12. $9y - 54$

EXERCISE 5h
(p. 66)

1. 2
2. 9
3. 1
4. 1
5. 4
6. 7
7. 2
8. 6

9. 1
10. 3
11. 2
12. 8
13. 2
14. 7

EXERCISE 5i
(p. 67)

1. 2.6 and 2.7
2. 5.2 and 5.3
3. 3.2 and 3.3
4. 5.5 and 5.6
5. 6.3 and 6.4
6. 1.5 and 1.6
7. 3.8 and 3.9
8. 3.3 and 3.4
9. 4.2 and 4.3
10. 4.1 and 4.2
11. 6.1 and 6.2
12. 4.6 and 4.7

CHAPTER 6 Enlargements

EXERCISE 6a
(p. 69)

Five millimetre squared paper is suitable for this exercise. To avoid pupils marking the text book, questions can be copied on squared paper and duplicated. Copymasters 77 and 78 in 5C provide extra practice.

9. a) 4 cm   b) 2 cm   d) 8 cm

EXERCISE 6b
(p. 71)

1. 4
2. 2
3. 3
4. 2

5. 12 cm
6. 15 cm by 24 cm
7. a) 20 cm   b) 12 cm
8. 7 cm

9. a) 2   b) 8 m
10. a) 3   b) 12 cm, 7.5 cm
11. a) 10   b) 5 m   c) 0.35 m

CHAPTER 7   Essential Geometry

This chapter revises the basic facts covered in books 1B and 2B. Pupils should not be expected to write out formal solutions but on the other hand a jumble of figures with the answer somewhere in the middle is most certainly unacceptable. Pupils should be expected to write the answer clearly at the end of any working, e.g. x is 50°.

EXERCISE 7a
(p. 76)

1. 70°	**4.** 35°	**7.** 130°	**10.** 138°
2. 140°	**5.** 130°	**8.** 30°	**11.** 38°
3. 65°	**6.** 90°	**9.** 40°	**12.** 52°

13. 300°	**14.** 50°	**15.** 180°	**16.** 55°

17. B	**18.** A	**19.** C	**20.** C	**21.** A

EXERCISE 7b
(p. 80)

1. 30°	**3.** 30°	**5.** 50°	**7.** 70°	**9.** 35°
2. 50°	**4.** 60°	**6.** 35°	**8.** 30°	**10.** 54°

11. 60°	**14.** 50°	**17.** 60°	**20.** 40°
12. 45°	**15.** 40°	**18.** 20°	**21.** 160°
13. 150°	**16.** 40°	**19.** 115°	**22.** 150°

EXERCISE 7c
(p. 84)

1. a) w	b) y	c) x	**3.** a) x	b) z	c) w
2. a) p	b) r	c) q	**4.** a) q	b) s	c) p

5. 120°	**8.** 100°
6. 110°	**9.** 60°
7. 50°	**10.** 110°

EXERCISE 7d
(p. 86)

1. 70°	**6.** $x = 120°, y = 100°$
2. $x = 55°, y = 55°$	**7.** $x = 120°$
3. $x = 80°, y = 100°$	**8.** $x = 70°, y = 70°, z = 110°$
4. $x = 140°, y = 40°$	**9.** $x = 80°, y = 30°, z = 70°$
5. $x = 60°, y = 60°$	**10.** $x = 70°, y = 70°$

EXERCISE 7e
(p. 87)

1. B	**4.** C	**7.** A
2. A	**5.** A	**8.** A
3. B	**6.** C	**9.** C

EXERCISE 7f
(p. 88)

For construction work, the emphasis should be on accuracy. Insist on a sharp pencil, but otherwise let the pupils use any instruments they like. Discuss how to draw an accurate right angle, how best to draw a line of given length and how to use a protractor. Question 1 is a good example to use for discussing the problems they may encounter.

(The diagrams given are half size.)

1. 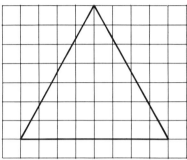 6.9 cm

2.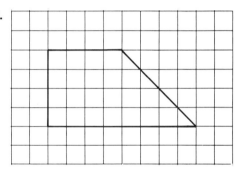
b) $x = 135°$
c) 135°

3.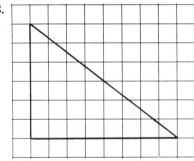
b) 10 cm

4.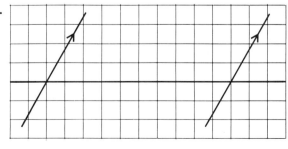
a) 60°

5.

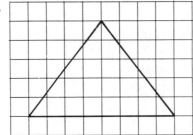

a) 50°
b) 80°
c) 80°

6.

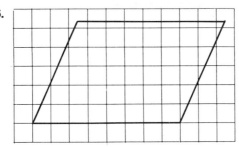

a) $x = 115°$
b) $y = 115°$
c) $z = 65°$

7.

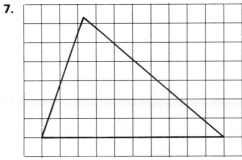

a) $x = 40°$
c) $y = 70°$
d) $y = 70°$

8.

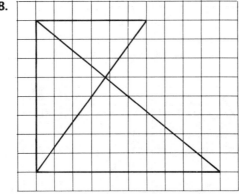

b) 38.5°
c) 53°

CHAPTER 8   Percentages

Exercises 8a and 8b revise and consolidate the meaning of percentage. Encourage instant conversion between decimal and percentage, e.g. 0.20 ⟺ 20%.
This is a long chapter and pupils could benefit if this were interspersed with other work, e.g. enlargements or transformations.

EXERCISE 8a
(p. 91)

1. 0.03	**6.** 0.16	**11.** 0.9	**16.** 0.2
2. 0.15	**7.** 0.44	**12.** 0.65	**17.** 0.81
3. 0.4	**8.** 0.5	**13.** 0.07	**18.** 1
4. 0.25	**9.** 0.24	**14.** 0.37	**19.** 0.3
5. 0.75	**10.** 0.05	**15.** 0.45	**20.** 0.28
21. 1.5	**24.** 3.2	**27.** 2.81	**30.** 1.20
22. 1.84	**25.** 3.42	**28.** 6	**31.** 2.00
23. 1.96	**26.** 4.07	**29.** 1.02	**32.** 2.50

EXERCISE 8b
(p. 92)

1. 62%	**4.** 205%	**7.** 540%	**10.** 30%	**13.** 25%
2. 11%	**5.** 3%	**8.** 10%	**11.** 80%	**14.** 75%
3. 187%	**6.** 130%	**9.** 70%	**12.** 32%	**15.** 150%

EXERCISE 8c
(p. 93)

1. 30%	**3.** 34%	**5.** 165%	**7.** 44%
2. 250%	**4.** 90%	**6.** 475%	**8.** 103%

EXERCISE 8d
(p. 93)

1. a) 0.24   b) 24%

2. a) $\frac{60}{100}$ or $\frac{3}{5}$ b) 0.6

3. a) $\frac{81}{100}$ b) 0.81

4.	$\frac{1}{2}$	50%	0.5
5.	$\frac{3}{4}$	75%	0.75
6.	$\frac{1}{4}$	25%	0.25
7.	$\frac{1}{5}$	20%	0.2
8.	$\frac{4}{5}$	80%	0.8

EXERCISE 8e
(p. 94)

1. 3%	**4.** 7%	**7.** 94%
2. 85%	**5.** 26%	**8.** 92%
3. 72%	**6.** 4%	**9.** 12%

EXERCISE 8f
(p. 95)

1. 2 p	**6.** £1	**11.** 60 cm
2. 60 m	**7.** 1 p	**12.** 567 km
3. 9 m	**8.** £12	**13.** £28
4. £8	**9.** 67.5 g	**14.** 6 mm
5. 12 cm	**10.** 27 m	**15.** 228 p

16. £6   **21.** 15 m   **26.** 40 m
17. 14 g   **22.** 2.4 km   **27.** 16 kg
18. £36   **23.** 2 p   **28.** 387 p
19. 6800 kg   **24.** 9 p   **29.** 16 m
20. 8 km   **25.** £4   **30.** 20 m

31. B   **32.** C   **33.** B

EXERCISE 8g   **1.** 4   **3.** 72   **5.** £385   **7.** 60 p   **9.** 15
(p. 96)   **2.** 63   **4.** 800   **6.** 588   **8.** 180   **10.** 7812

EXERCISE 8h   **1.** 20%   **3.** 25%   **5.** 4%   **7.** 20%
(p. 97)   **2.** 32%   **4.** 30%   **6.** 30%   **8.** 90%

                   9. 64%   **12.** 25%   **15.** 20%   **18.** 30%
                   10. 48%   **13.** 25%   **16.** 8%   **19.** 50%
                   11. 130% **14.** 10%   **17.** $37\frac{1}{2}$% **20.** 85%

EXERCISE 8i   **1.** 4%   **3.** 4%   **5.** 2%   **7.** 20%
(p. 98)   **2.** 20%   **4.** 12%   **6.** 20%   **8.** 19%

                   9. 42.9% **12.** 27.3% **15.** 62.5% **18.** 22.2%
                   10. 66.7% **13.** 58.8% **16.** 77.8% **19.** 18.2%
                   11. 2%   **14.** 83.3% **17.** 133.3% **20.** 17.1%

EXERCISE 8j   **1.** 48%   **5.** 95%
(p. 100)   **2.** 20%   **6.** 8%
                   3. 37.5%; 62.5%   **7.** 66.7%
                   4. 32%   **8.** 24%

EXERCISE 8k   **1.** £1.80   **5.** £42
(p. 101)   **2.** £19.75   **6.** 16 p
                   3. £14.40   **7.** £375
                   4. £42

                   8. £99   **10.** £127.50
                   9. £528   **11.** £237.50

                   12. £18   **14.** £192, £448
                   13. £36

EXERCISE 8l   **1.** 80 p   **6.** £600
(p. 103)   **2.** £2560   **7.** 190 cm
                   3. £12 000; £52 000 **8.** £190.40
                   4. £49; £189   **9.** £3.18
                   5. £32   **10.** £96

	11. 50%	16. 60%
	12. 42.9%	17. 16.7%
	13. 33.3%	18. 10%
	14. 5%	19. 19%
	15. 20%	

EXERCISE 8m
(p. 106)

1. £29.90	3. £14.26	5. £65.09	7. £1840
2. £71.30	4. £14.72	6. £55.66	8. £7360

EXERCISE 8n
(p. 107)

1. a) $\frac{8}{100}$ or $\frac{2}{25}$ b) 0.08   5. 195
2. a) 0.6   b) 60%   6. 92%
3. 18 p   7. 7%
4. 132%   8. £360

EXERCISE 8p
(p. 107)

1. 0.26	3. £3.30	5. 91%	7. 20%	9. 35%
2. 65%	4. 0.37	6. 2 days	8. 20%	10. £21.39

EXERCISE 8q
(p. 108)

1. C	3. B	5. C	7. A
2. C	4. D	6. D	8. B

CHAPTER 9   Probability

The technical language used in this topic often leads to misunderstanding: the words "event", "outcome", "random", "possibility", etc. all have precise meanings and these meanings need to be made clear with plenty of discussion. It is advisable to have some packs of cards and some dice available. (We have used the plural form, dice, for one die. This is deliberate as it is the word used by most people including some examination boards, but it is a good idea to tell pupils that the singular is die.)

EXERCISE 9a
(p. 109)

This revises the work covered in books 1B and 2B.

1. a) 4   b) 2   c) 0.5
2. a) 5   b) 2   c) 0.4   d) 0
3. a) 0.17   b) 0.33   c) 0   d) 1   e) 0.33   f) 0
4. They are equally likely.

EXERCISE 9b
(p. 111)

Numbers 10 to 14 can be used for discussion with everyone.

1. $\frac{3}{5}$	3. $\frac{21}{26}$	5. $\frac{7}{10}$	7. $\frac{24}{25}$	9. $\frac{39}{40}$
2. $\frac{12}{13}$	4. $\frac{5}{6}$	6. $\frac{5}{8}$	8. $\frac{2}{3}$	10. $\frac{10}{13}$

11. a) $\frac{1}{10}$ b) $\frac{3}{10}$ c) $\frac{2}{5}$ d) $\frac{7}{10}$
12. a) $\frac{1}{13}$ b) $\frac{1}{4}$ c) $\frac{3}{4}$ d) $\frac{11}{13}$
13. a) $\frac{15}{22}$ b) $\frac{7}{22}$ c) $\frac{1}{22}$ d) $\frac{3}{11}$
14. a) $\frac{2}{5}$ b) $\frac{19}{30}$ c) $\frac{7}{30}$ d) 0

EXERCISE 9c
(p. 114)

1.

	1st bag				
	○	○	○	●	●
○	(○,○)	(○,○)	(○,○)	(○,●)	(○,●)
○	(○,○)	(○,○)	(○,○)	(○,●)	(○,●)
2nd bag ○	(○,○)	(○,○)	(○,○)	(○,●)	(○,●)
●	(●,○)	(●,○)	(●,○)	(●,●)	(●,●)
●	(●,○)	(●,○)	(●,○)	(●,●)	(●,●)

2.

			Dice				
		1	2	3	4	5	6
10 p	H	(H,1)	(H,2)	(H,3)	(H,4)	(H,5)	(H,6)
	T	(T,1)	(T,2)	(T,3)	(T,4)	(T,5)	(T,6)

3.

		1st bag			
		R	R	Y	B
	R	(R,R)	(R,R)	(R,Y)	(R,B)
2nd bag	Y	(Y,R)	(Y,R)	(Y,Y)	(Y,B)
	Y	(Y,R)	(Y,R)	(Y,Y)	(Y,B)
	B	(B,R)	(B,R)	(B,Y)	(B,B)

4.

		1st spin		
		1	2	3
	1	(1,1)	(1,2)	(1,3)
2nd spin	2	(2,1)	(2,2)	(2,3)
	3	(3,1)	(3,2)	(3,3)

5.

		Pencil		
		Red	Green	Yellow
	Round	Round, Red	Round, Green	Round, Yellow
Rubber	Square	Square, Red	Square, Green	Square, Yellow
	Triangular	Triangular, Red	Triangular, Green	Triangular, Yellow

EXERCISE 9d
(p. 116)

1. a) 0.11   b) 0.17   c) 0.17   d) 0.83

2. a) 0.12   b) 0.64

3. 0.07

4. a) 0.06   b) 0.13   c) 0.19   d) 0.63

5.

		5 p coin	
		H	T
1 p coin	H	(H, H)	(H, T)
	T	(T, H)	(T, T)

0.25

6.

		1st dice					
		1	●	3	4	●	6
2nd dice	1	(1, 1)	(1, ●)	(1, 3)	(1, 4)	(1, ●)	(1, 6)
	2	(2, 1)	(2, ●)	(2, 3)	(2, 4)	(2, ●)	(2, 6)
	3	(3, 1)	(3, ●)	(3, 3)	(3, 4)	(3, ●)	(3, 6)
	4	(4, 1)	(4, ●)	(4, 3)	(4, 4)	(4, ●)	(4, 6)
	5	(5, 1)	(5, ●)	(5, 3)	(5, 4)	(5, ●)	(5, 6)
	6	(6, 1)	(6, ●)	(6, 3)	(6, 4)	(6, ●)	(6, 6)

a) 0.14   b) 0.06   c) 0.06   d) 0.53

7.

		1st bag				
		10 p	10 p	10 p	50 p	50 p
2nd bag	10 p	(10 p, 10 p)	(10 p, 10 p)	(10 p, 10 p)	(10 p, 50 p)	(10 p, 50 p)
	50 p	(50 p, 10 p)	(50 p, 10 p)	(50 p, 10 p)	(50 p, 50 p)	(50 p, 50 p)

0.2

8.

		1st shelf				
		Story	Story	Text	Text	Text
2nd shelf	Story	(S, S)	(S, S)	(S, T)	(S, T)	(S, T)
	Story	(S, S)	(S, S)	(S, T)	(S, T)	(S, T)
	Story	(S, S)	(S, S)	(S, T)	(S, T)	(S, T)
	Text	(T, S)	(T, S)	(T, T)	(T, T)	(T, T)

a) 0.3   b) 0.15

9. a) 0.25   b) 0.06   c) 0.75   d) 0.25

CHAPTER 10   Formulae

This chapter concentrates on using formulae and involves substituting positive numbers into formulae. The last section deals with making formulae by first making a flow chart; this form of flow chart was called a function machine in books 1B and 2B and the use of the new name needs pointing out.

EXERCISE 10a   **1.** 10   **2.** 6   **3.** 14   **4.** 4
(p. 120)

5. 15   **7.** 8   **9.** a) 16   b) 77   c) 8.2
6. 19   **8.** 8   **10.** a) 14   b) 11.2   c) 0.96

11. 16   **13.** 19   **15.** 27   **17.** 10
12. 16   **14.** 15   **16.** 10

18. a) 9.9   b) $a = 3, b = 4, c = 5$ c) 12   d) 12 cm
e) 15, 30 and 25 *or* 1.5, 3 and 2.5
19. a) £380   b) $n = 120, t = 4$; £760
20. a) $v = 55, t = 3.5$ b) 192.5 km   c) 147 km

21. C   **22.** D   **23.** A   **24.** B   **25.** A

EXERCISE 10b   Remind pupils of the meaning of terms such as $2x^2$.
(p. 123)
1. 6   **2.** 24   **3.** 6   **4.** 49   **5.** 36

6. 36   **8.** 18   **10.** 18
7. 54   **9.** 45   **11.** 18

12. 3   **13.** 3   **14.** 3   **15.** $\frac{2}{7}$

16. 147   **17.** 5   **18.** $\frac{1}{2}$ **19.** 24

20. a) 2   b) 4   c) 4 cm^2
21. a) 12   b) 144   c) 144 mm^2
22. a) 1.5   b) 2.25   c) 2.25 m^2
23. $l = 6, b = 3, h = 3$ b) 54 m^2
24. 10 cm   **25.** 370 p

26. a) L = 80, E = 25   b) 3.2
27. a) L = 40, E = 15   b) 2.67
28. 12.5

29. B   **30.** B   **31.** D

EXERCISE 10c   These give simple linear equations which can often be solved by guesswork.
(p. 127)

1. 4	**2.** 7	**3.** 4	**4.** 4	**5.** 5
6. 2	**7.** 2	**8.** 4	**9.** 7	**10.** 3

EXERCISE 10d   **1.** a)
(p. 129)

b) 560 p   c) $C = 70n$

2. a)

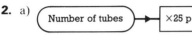

b) 150 p   c) $C = 25n$

3. a)

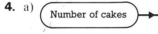

b) 52   c) $y = x - 4$

4. a)

Number of cakes → ×24 p → Total cost

b) 144 p   c) $C = 24n$

5. a)

Number of pupils → ×2 → Number of exercise books

b) 150   c) $N = 2n$

6. a) 5   b) $T = n + 1$

7. a) 3 hours   b) $H = n + 1$

8. a)

Number of pupils → ×2 → +10 → Number of sheets

b) 40   c) $N = 2n + 10$

9. a) 450 p   b) $C = n \times d$

10. a) 5   b) $m = (a + b + c) \div 3$

CHAPTER 11   Plans and Elevations

This work is useful in making the pupils think about the shape of an object, how it is constructed and how it looks when viewed from different directions. Three-dimensional models are needed. Some may be going on to further study of Design and Realisation but even those who are not will benefit.

You may decide that sketching and drawing on squared paper is all that is required and leave the accurate drawing with instruments to the graphics classes.

EXERCISE 11a **1.** a) none   b) west elevation   c)
(p. 133)

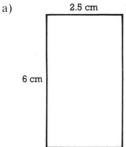

2. a)

2.5 cm

6 cm

b)

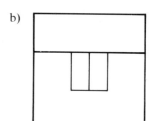

2.5 cm

6 cm

2 cm

3. a)

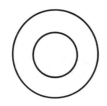

b)

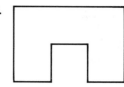

EXERCISE 11b **1.** a) C   b) E   c) G
(p. 137)

2.

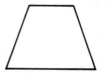

3.

4. a)

b)

The elevation is the same from any direction.

5. It would be a good idea to have a large scale model of this solid.
   a) B   b) E

EXERCISE 11c
(p. 140)

The diagrams in this exercise and the next are drawn half-size.

1.

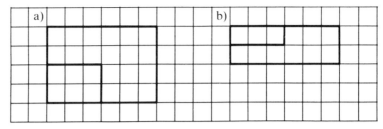

2.

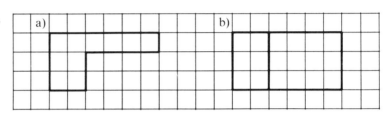

3.

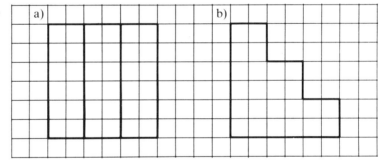

4.

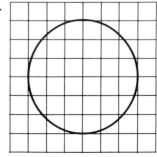

5.

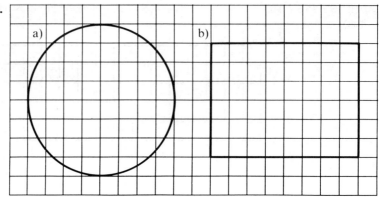

EXERCISE 11d   At the end of this book there is a copymaster with two extra questions
(p. 143)   which could usefully be completed before attempting this exercise.

1.

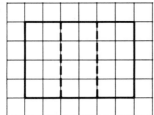

4.

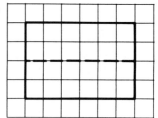

2.

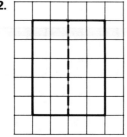

5.

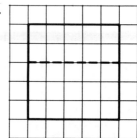

3.

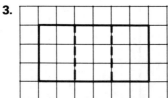

6.

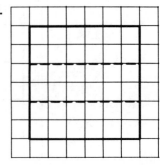

7. 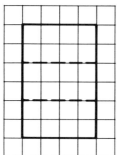   **8.**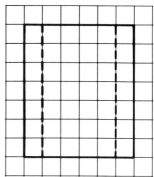

9.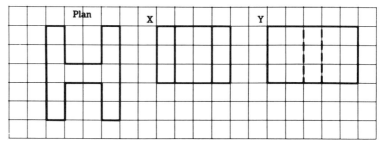

10.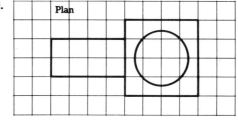

CHAPTER 12   Speed and other Compound Units

Pupils frequently forget the relationship between speed, distance and time; it will need reinforcing several times.

EXERCISE 12a **1.** 4 mph   **3.** 32 mph   **5.** 1250 mph
(p. 145)   **2.** 10 mph   **4.** 250 mph   **6.** 55 mph

7. 2 m/s   **9.** 45 km/h   **11.** 2 m/h
8. 6 m/s   **10.** 1020 km/h   **12.** 30 m/s

EXERCISE 12b **1.** 4 km/h   **3.** 42 mph   **5.** 98 km/h
(p. 146)   **2.** 11 mph   **4.** 250 mph   **6.** 4.5 m/s

7. A   **8. D**   **9. D**   **10. D**

11. 42 km/h   **13.** 12 km/h   **15.** 80 mph   **17.** 2.8 m/s
12. 4 mph   **14.** 162 mph   **16.** 8 m/s

EXERCISE 12c **1.** 9.5 km/h   **5.** 32 mph   **9.** 6.5 mph
(p. 149)   **2.** 3 mph   **6.** 700 km/h   **10.** 120 m/s
                  3. 90 km/h   **7.** 20 km/h   **11.** 28 m/s
                  4. 5 m/s   **8.** 60 km/h   **12.** 180 mph

EXERCISE 12d **1.** 120 miles   **3.** 15 miles   **5.** 29.7 m
(p. 150)   **2.** 40 km   **4.** 6875 km

6. 100 minutes   **9.** 150 minutes   **12.** 7.5 km   **14.** 6.75 km
7. 55 seconds   **10.** 372 minutes   **13.** 17 hours   **15.** 2.5 seconds
8. 14 hours   **11.** 36 km/h

16. 175 miles   **18.** 14 miles   **20.** 28 km
17. 4 km   **19.** 33 km

EXERCISE 12e **1.** 3400 cm^3 **3.** 250 cm^3 **5.** 5 cm^3
(p. 154)   **2.** 2650 cm^3 **4.** 14 000 cm^3 **6.** 73 cm^3

7. 4 ℓ   **9.** 0.8 ℓ   **11.** 7ℓ
8. 8 ℓ   **10.** 43 ℓ   **12.** 0.5 ℓ

13. 500 cm^3 **15.** 300 mℓ   **17.** 250 mℓ
14. 1500 mℓ   **16.** 2.5 ℓ   **18.** 5000 cm^3

EXERCISE 12f **1.** a) 50 g   b) 5000 g   c) 4 m^2
(p. 155)   **2.** a) 20 kg   b) 2000 kg   c) 50 m^2

3. a) 10 m^2 b) 20 m^2 c) 5 m^2
4. a) 6 m^2 b) 6 m^2/ℓ

5. 20 m^2 **8.** 12.5
6. 3810 g   **9.** a) 40 mℓ   b) 400 mℓ   c) 12.5 ℓ
7. a) 3000 kg   b) 25 m^2 **10.** 5 rolls

EXERCISE 12g **(p. 157)**	**1.** 1.25 g/cm^3 **2.** 0.84 g/cm^3 **3.** 133.3 kg/cm^3 **4.** 11.4 g/cm^3 **5.** 19.1 g/cm^3 **6.** a) 3300 g b) 1.1 g/cm^3 **7.** a) 1000 g b) 2.5 g/cm^3		**8.** a) 1.05 kg b) 4.2 kg **9.** 0.25 m^3 **10.** a) 1000 cm^3 b) 0.2 g/cm^3 **11.** a) 4.2 g b) 19.05 cm^3 **12.** 400 cm^3 **13.** 81 g **12.** 75 kg

EXERCISE 12h **(p. 159)**	**1.** 200 miles **2.** 3000 ℓ **3.** 40 hours **4.** 60 seconds	**5.** 60 ℓ **6.** 200 km **7.** The question cannot be answered because no information is given about the speed. **8.** 4800 lb

CHAPTER 13   Quadrilaterals, Polygons and Tessellations

EXERCISE 13a **(p. 161)**	**1.** $p = 64°$ **2.** $q = 135°$ **3.** $r = 90°$ **4.** $s = 88°$	**5.** $t = 73°, 2t = 146°$ **6.** $u = 94°$ **7.** $v = 90°$ **8.** $x = 36°, 2x = 72°, 3x = 108°, 4x = 144°$

EXERCISE 13b
(p. 163)

The first two questions in this exercise give the opportunity for plenty of discussion of the many different places where squares and rectangles are found in everyday life.

1. (a), (d), (e), (f), (g) and (h) are rectangles
   (b) and (c) are squares
4. a) each is 6 cm
   b) each is 90°
   c) all four sides are equal
   d) AB is parallel to DC and AD is parallel to BC
   e) a square
5. a) AB = 8 cm, BC = 5 cm, DC = 8 cm, AD = 5 cm
   b) each is 90°
   c) AB = DC and AD = BC
   d) AB is parallel to DC and AD is parallel to BC
   e) a rectangle

Pupils find it surprisingly difficult to remember which name refers to which quadrilateral, and will need frequent reminders. A copymaster with further examples on this work is included at the end of this book and can be used later for revision.

EXERCISE 13c **(p. 167)**	**1.** a) all the sides are equal **2.** a) no two sides are equal	b) a rhombus b) a trapezium

3. a) SP = SR and PQ = QR   b) a kite
4. a) WX = ZY and WZ = XY   b) a parallelogram

EXERCISE 13d
(p. 167)

1. rectangle
2. trapezium
3. parallelogram
4. general quadrilateral
5. rectangle
6. kite
7. kite
8. rectangle
9. square
10. rhombus
11. parallelogram
12. trapezium

EXERCISE 13e
(p. 169)

1. a) parallelogram   b) $x = 80°, y = z = 100°$
2. a) rhombus   b) $x = z = 75°, y = 105°$
3. a) parallelogram   b) $x = y = 65°, z = 115°$
4. a) rhombus   b) $x = 45°, y = z = 135°$
5. a) square, trapezium   b) $x = y = 90°, z = 45°$
6. a) parallelogram, trapezium   b) $x = 130°, y = 50°, z = 40°$
7. a) parallelogram, rectangle, trapezium
   b) $x = 35°, y = 90°, z = 35°$
8. a) trapezium, trapezium   b) $x = 60°, y = 120°, z = 60°$

9. $x = 105°$
10. $y = 100°, z = 100°$
11. $p = 115°, q = 90°$
12. $r = 112°, s = 108°$
13. $t = 102°$
14. $u = 98°, v = 55°$
15. $w = 125°, x = 60°$
16. $e = 135°, f = 70°, g = 85°$

EXERCISE 13f
(p. 172)

Use question 8 for discussion: accept the answer "no" because a circle does not have straight sides, but if anyone brings it up, discuss the idea of a circle being a polygon with a very large number of very small sides. Do not take the discussion further to include the idea of a limit – this is too sophisticated an idea.

1. no   **3.** no   **5.** no   **7.** yes
2. yes   **4.** no   **6.** no   **8.** no

EXERCISE 13g
(p. 173)

1. 3   **3.** 5   **5.** 8
2. 6   **4.** 9   **6.** 12

7. 120°, 60°, 72°, 40°, 45°, 30°
8. a) 7   b) 15

EXERCISE 13i
(p. 175)

1. a) $p = 130°, q = 120°, r = 110°$ b) 360°
2. a) $p = 110°, r = 130°, s = 50°, t = 70°$ b) 360°
3. a) $m = 90°, n = 90°, p = 30°, q = 90°, r = 60°$ b) 360°
4. 360°

EXERCISE 13j
(p. 177)

1. 40°   **3.** 60°   **5.** 50°   **7.** 110°
2. 60°   **4.** 100°   **6.** 40°   **8.** 50°

9. a) 360°   b) yes, they are all equal   c) 60°
10. a) 360°   b) yes, they are all equal   c) 72°
11. a) 360°   b) yes, they are all equal   c) 45°
12. a) 360°   b) yes, they are all equal   c) 30°
13. a) 18°   b) 162°
14. a) 120°   b) 108°
15. 18
16. 40°

EXERCISE 13k   **1.** 540°   **3.** 720°   **5.** 1800°
(p. 181)   **2.** 1440°   **4.** 360°   **6.** 1080°

7. a) 540°   b) 80°   **11.** a) 720°   b) 110°
8. a) 540°   b) 120°   **12.** a) 720°   b) 60°
9. a) 360°   b) 80°   **13.** a) 900°   b) 140°
10. a) 540°   b) 130°   **14.** a) 720°   b) 120°

15. a) 72°   b) 108°   **19.** a) 36°   b) 144°
16. a) 60°   b) 120°   **20.** a) 30°   b) 150°
17. a) 45°   b) 135°   **21.** a) 18°   b) 162°
18. a) 90°   b) 90°   **22.** a) 120°   b) 60°

EXERCISE 13l   The template made for question 5 can be used to draw the net for a
(p. 184)   regular dodecahedron:

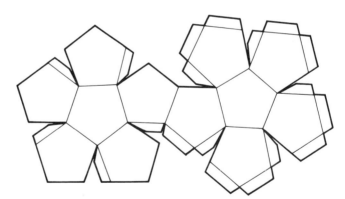

This model needs a very accurate net or it will not work, so only pupils
who can draw accurately should do it.

1.

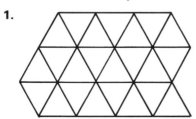

5. a) no   b) a regular 10-sided polygon

6. a) the interior angles are too big   b) a square

EXERCISE 13m   Copymaster 36 from *5C Copymasters* gives some extra practice in
(p. 187)   tessellations of two shapes.

CHAPTER 14   More Equations and Formulae

EXERCISE 14a (p. 189)			
1. 6	**4.** 6	**7.** 15	**10.** 7
2. 7	**5.** 4	**8.** 8	**11.** 4
3. 1	**6.** 5	**9.** 5	**12.** 0

EXERCISE 14b (p. 190)			
1. 4	**4.** 2	**7.** 5	**10.** 3
2. 1	**5.** 1	**8.** 2	**11.** 3
3. 2	**6.** 4	**9.** 4	**12.** 4

EXERCISE 14c (p. 191)			
1. A; 4	**4.** C; 7	**7.** A (or B); 6	**10.** A; 5
2. C; 4	**5.** B; 2	**8.** B; 3	**11.** A or B; 5
3. A (or B); 6	**6.** A (or C); 6	**9.** C; 2	**12.** B; 1
13. 4	**16.** 2	**19.** 4	**22.** 4
14. 5	**17.** 28	**20.** 5	**23.** 5
15. 4	**18.** 3	**21.** 8	**24.** 23

EXERCISE 14d
(p. 191)

1. 8

2. 4

3. 2

4. 2

5. a) 10   b) 6   c) 3

6. a) 8   b) 7   c) 4

7. a) 228   b) 354   c) 10

8. a) 40   b) 33   c) 10

CHAPTER 15   Bearings

When introducing this topic make use of the directions of certain well-known landmarks in relation to the classroom and/or the position of the most important local feature.

A large cardboard compass with a moveable needle is useful for demonstration purposes but show pupils a real compass so that they can relate to actual situations.

EXERCISE 15a
(p. 193)

Copymaster 83 from 5C can also be used for this work.

1. a) NE   b) SW   c) due west

2. bus stop   **3.** NW   **4.** due east

5. NE	**8.** SE	**11.** due east
6. due north	**9.** farm	**12.** NE
7. church	**10.** due north	**13.** SW

14. pine	**17.** ash	**20.** oak and sycamore
15. walnut	**18.** 90° anticlockwise or 270° clockwise	**21.** ash
16. 90°	**19.** walnut	**22.** sycamore

EXERCISE 15b
(p. 196)

1.

5.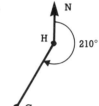

2.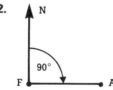

6.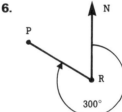

3.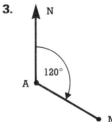

7.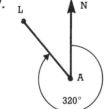

4.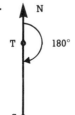

8.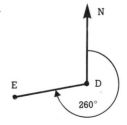

9.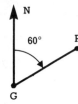

12.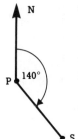

10.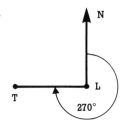

13.

11.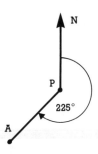

14.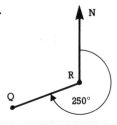

EXERCISE 15c
(p. 198)

1. 080°   **3.** 020°   **5.** 090°
2. 130°   **4.** 106°   **6.** 180°

7. 270°   **9.** 320°   **11.** 350°
8. 205°   **10.** 256°   **12.** 190°

13.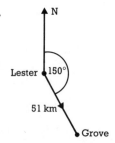

14.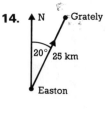

15.

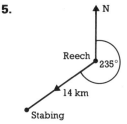

17.

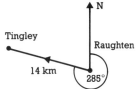

16.

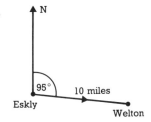

EXERCISE 15d The copymasters supplied at the end of this book for this and the
(p. 200) following exercise can be used for further questions; extra place names
can be added if required. Copymasters 86–88 from 5C provide more
questions on bearings.

1. b) 17°   c) 017°
2. b) 152°   c) 152°
3. b) 68°   c) 068°
4. b) 90°   c) 090°   d) East

5. b) 248°   **7.** b) 218°
6. b) 332°   **8.** b) 270°

EXERCISE 15e **1.** 150°   **3.** 158°   **5.** 215°
(p. 202)   **2.** 072°   **4.** 214°

6. false   **7.** true   **8.** false   **9.** true

CHAPTER 16   Inequalities ▬▬▬▬▬▬▬▬▬▬▬▬▬▬

EXERCISE 16a **1.** true   **4.** true   **7.** false
(p. 204)   **2.** false   **5.** true   **8.** true
3. true   **6.** true   **9.** false

10. >   **13.** <   **16.** <   **19.** <   **22.** <
11. >   **14.** >   **17.** >   **20.** >   **23.** >
12. >   **15.** <   **18.** <   **21.** <

EXERCISE 16b
(p. 206)

Use is made in this chapter of closed and open circles to indicate whether or not the value at the end of a range is included in the range. Some teachers may feel that this can be ignored at this level and can give pupils the appropriate advice.

A copymaster with several blank number lines is given at the end of this book. *Two copies* of it are needed to complete the exercise.

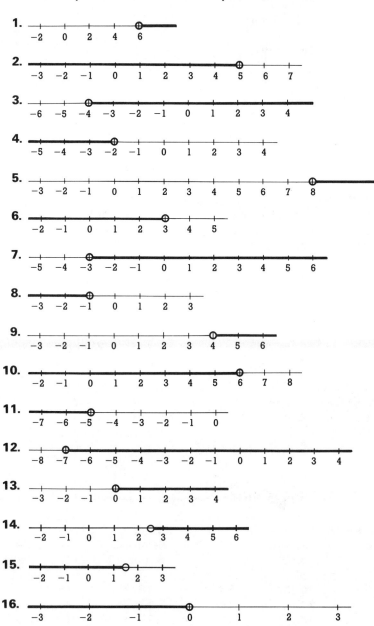

17.
-2 -1 0 1 2 3

18.
-3 -2 -1 0 1

19.
-2   -1   0   1   2   3

20.
-4 -3 -2 -1 0 1 2 3

21.
-4 -3 -2 -1 0 1 2 3

22. a) $x < 0$ b)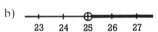
-2 -1 0 1 2

23. a) $x > 20$ b)
18 19 20 21 22

24. a) $x > 25$ b)
23 24 25 26 27

EXERCISE 16c (p. 207)	**1.** yes	**4.** no	**7.** yes	**10.** yes
	2. yes	**5.** no	**8.** yes	**11.** yes
	3. yes	**6.** no	**9.** yes	**12.** yes

EXERCISE 16d (p. 208)   (Example answers given.)

1. 6, 10	**4.** 6, 8	**7.** 3, 5	**10.** 3, 1
2. -2, 0	**5.** -5, -10	**8.** -6, -3	**11.** -2, 0
3. -5, -8	**6.** 0, 1	**9.** -10, -15	**12.** 0, -2

EXERCISE 16e (p. 208)

1. 13	**3.** 1	**5.** 21
2. -3	**4.** -17	**6.** -8

7. 7	**9.** -6	**11.** 17
8. -1	**10.** -11	**12.** -16

13. 11	**15.** 11	**17.** 23
14. 5	**16.** 19	**18.** 31

19. 7	**21.** 19	**23.** 23
20. 7	**22.** 2	**24.** 29

25. 25	**27.** 30	**29.** 70	**31.** 30
26. 42	**28.** 48	**30.** 30	**32.** 120

EXERCISE 16f (p. 211)

1. $6 > 0$	**6.** $3 < 7$
2. $11 < 16$	**7.** $-1 < 6$
3. $2 > -7$	**8.** $9 > 3$
4. $-1 < 4$	**9.** $-1 < 3$
5. $-2 < 3$	**10.** $-9 < -8$

Although we have not spelled it out, pupils are actually solving inequalities in the following questions. Some teachers may consider mentioning this and perhaps developing the idea a little.

11. $x > 9$

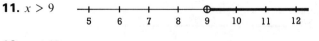

12. $x < 17$

13. $x > 9$

14. $x > 3$

15. $x < 8$

16. $x > -4$

17. $x < 3$

18. $x < -13$

EXERCISE 16g **1.** $x \geqslant 6$ **3.** $x \geqslant 5$ **5.** $x \leqslant 6$
(p. 213)   **2.** $x \leqslant 50$ **4.** $x \geqslant -5$

EXERCISE 16h **1.** $x \geqslant 3$ and $x < 20$
(p. 214)

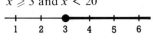

2. $x \geqslant 80$ and $x \leqslant 305$

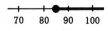
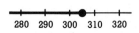

3. $x > 100$ and $x \leqslant 250$

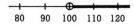
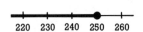

4. $x \geqslant 7$ and $x \leqslant 15$

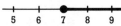

5. $7 < N < 19$

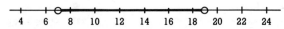

6. $5 \leqslant X \leqslant 13$

7. $3 \leqslant N \leqslant 8$

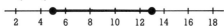

8. $8 < x \leqslant 12$

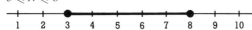

9. $30 \leqslant x \leqslant 80$

10. $26 \leqslant x < 40$

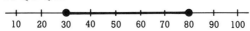

EXERCISE 16i
(p. 216)

1. a) $-2° > -9°$ b) $5° > -6°$ c) $4° > -1°$
2. a) yes   b) yes
3. $-5, -6$ etc.
4. a) 8   b) -4
5. a) 11   b) -6
6. $x \geqslant 100$
7.

8. $12 \leqslant x \leqslant 16$

EXERCISE 16j
(p. 217)

1. a)   b)
2. a) false   b) true   c) false
3. 4, 5 etc.
4. a) $11 > 1$ b) $-7 < 3$ c) $x > 7$
5. a) $N < 5$ b) $N \geqslant 2$ c) $N \leqslant 10$
6. $N \leqslant 8$
7.
8. a) $-2 < N < 3$ b) $-8 \leqslant N \leqslant -1$ c) $3 < N \leqslant 14$

CHAPTER 17   Grouping and Displaying Data

The first two exercises revise the work in books 1B and 2B. Throughout this chapter, data extracted from existing databases within the school can be used to supplement, or even replace, information given in the exercises.

Very large quantities of information can then be handled as the data can be presented in order; consequently grouping and counting the data become much easier.

EXERCISE 17a
(p. 220) Question 2(f) is deliberate – it should be used for discussion to show that when information is processed, not all questions can be answered and that some details get lost.

1. a) 3 and 4   b) 6

2. a) 9   b) 5   c)

Type of pet	Dog	Cat	Bird	Other pet
Frequency	9	8	5	7

d) 29   e) rabbit, hamster, . . .   f) it is not possible to answer this

3. a)

Category	M	W	B	G
Frequency	10	9	6	7

c) 16 males, 16 females   d) 1

4. a)

Number of rooms	1	2	3	4	5	6	7
Frequency	2	2	4	4	7	6	5

c) 5   d) 140

EXERCISE 17b
(p. 222) (Bar charts are included with the answers to give an idea of the shape: they are not fully labelled.)

1. a) $3\frac{1}{2}$–4
   b) no (as soon as data is grouped, some details are lost and this should be made clear whenever the opportunity arises)

2. a)

Mark	30–39	40–49	50–59	60–69	70–79	80–89
Frequency	8	11	18	13	8	12

b)

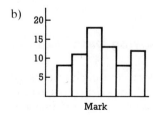

Mark

3. a)

No. of words	1–5	6–10	11–15	16–20	21–25	26–29
Frequency	1	3	8	5	5	2

b)

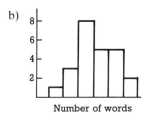

Number of words

EXERCISE 17c
(p. 223)

1. whole number
2. continuous
3. whole number

4. continuous
5. continuous
6. continuous

EXERCISE 17d
(p. 224)

The notation that we have used for groups of continuous data is easy to understand and quick to write but it relies on the understanding that each group is the same width, thus implying the upper boundary of the last group. An alternative notation, e.g. height h cm: $130 \leqslant h < 135$ etc., avoids this problem but, in our view, its complexity outweighs the value of its rigour!

1. a) 8   b) 4   c) 140 cm to less than 145 cm

d)

Height	Frequency
130 –	8
135 –	14
140 –	18
145 –	12
150 –	5
Total	57

2. a) 1   b) 7   c) 20   d) no

3. a) 47 kg   b) 5   c)

Weight	Frequency
40 –	20
60 –	61
80 –	13
100 –	6
Total	100

d) 6   e) 81

EXERCISE 17e
(p. 226)

1.

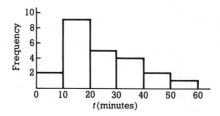

2.

Weight (in kg)	4 –	8 –	12 –
Tally	ⵑⵑ ‖	ⵑⵑⵑⵑ ‖	ⵑⵑ ‖
Frequency	7	12	7

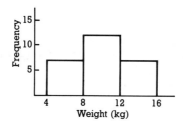

3.

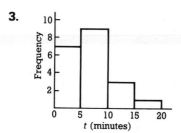

4.

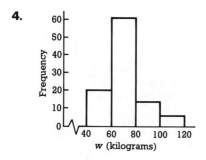

5. a) sensible groups would be 50–<55, 55–<60, . . . , 75–<80

b) (This bar chart uses the groups suggested in (a)).

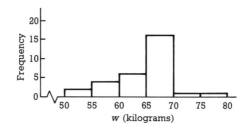

EXERCISE 17f
(p. 228)

1. a) tubs   b) cornets   c) choc ices and orange lollies

2. a) red   b) yellow   c) blue and purple

3. a) form time   b) PE and meals and breaks

4. a) $\frac{1}{4}$ b) $\frac{1}{12}$ c) £45   d) £15   e) £120

5. a) $\frac{1}{4}$ b) $\frac{1}{6}$ c) 90   d) 60   e) 150

6. a) $\frac{1}{4}$ b) 21   c) 25   d) 26

7. a) $\frac{5}{12}$ b) 65   c) 7

EXERCISE 17g
(p. 232)

The method that we have used for calculating the angle required for each slice is suitable whether or not the angle is a whole number of degrees. If all the examples the pupils are given lead to uncomplicated angles the alternative method, finding the angle that represents one item, is suitable.

In the example discussed in preparation for Exercise 18e we could say that one piece is represented by $\dfrac{360°}{24}$ i.e. 15°. Hence the number of plates is represented by $7 \times 15°$. All the questions in Exercise 18e can be done by this method.

1. grey, 96°; blue, 48°; brown, 168°; hazel, 48°.

2. bus, 144°; car, 84°; bicycle, 36°; walking, 60°; other, 36°.

3. science, maths 90°; art, music 60°; English 40°; languages 60°; others 110°.

4. total viewing time was 30 hours.
comedy series, 180°; news, 12°; plays and films, 60°; documentaries, 60°; other programmes, 48°.

5. soccer, 108°; tennis, 72°; cricket, 90°; snooker, 54°; other sports, 36°.

EXERCISE 17h   **1.** a)
(p. 234)

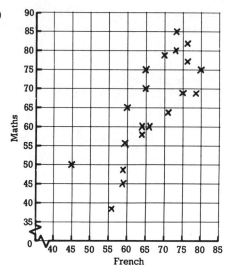

b) yes

2. a)

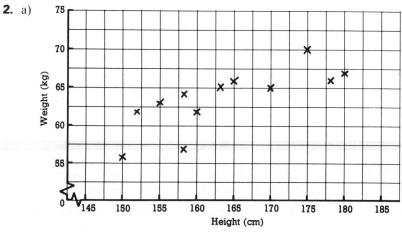

b) fairly likely

3. a)

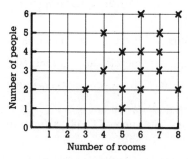

b) too much scatter to give an opinion

4. a)

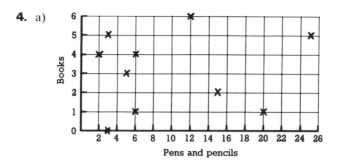

b) no

EXERCISE 17i
(p. 237)
Allow plenty of leeway when judging a line of best fit: one method of locating this line a bit more accurately is to find the mean values of the two quantities and to use these values as the coordinates of a point on the line; however, at this stage, this is likely to complicate a simple idea. If you have appropriate software, illustrating one of these questions on a computer is worthwhile.

1. strong, moderate, weak, none (allow some leeway)

CHAPTER 18   Ratio and Proportion

EXERCISE 18a
(p. 238)

1. 5 compared with 1
2. 4 compared with 3
3. 3 compared with 2

4. 3 compared with 1
5. 4 compared with 3
6. 5 compared with 3

EXERCISE 18b
(p. 239)

1. 10 cm : 6 cm = 5 : 3
2. 15 p : 5 p = 3 : 1
3. £24 : £12 = 2 : 1
4. 72 cm : 27 cm = 8 : 3
5. 8 kg : 14 kg = 4 : 7

6. 1. £10 : £2 = 5 : 1
 2. 8 m : 6 m = 4 : 3
 3. 15 kg : 10 kg = 3 : 2
 4. 36 p : 12 p = 3 : 1
 5. 24 g : 18 g = 4 : 3
 6. 40 m : 24 m = 5 : 3

7. £18 compared with £12 is the same as 3 compared with 2.
8. 42 cm compared with 28 cm is the same as 3 compared with 2.
9. 16 cm compared with 24 cm is the same as 2 compared with 3.
10. 18 g compared with 20 g is the same as 9 compared with 10.

EXERCISE 18c
(p. 240)

1. 4 : 5
2. 1 : 2
3. 2 : 1
4. 2 : 3

5. 7 : 5
6. 3 : 1
7. 6 : 5
8. 3 : 4

9. 3 : 2
10. 3 : 2
11. 4 : 3
12. 4 : 9

13. 3 : 4
14. 3 : 7
15. 3 : 2
16. 9 : 5

17. 4 : 9
18. 2 : 3
19. 5 : 8
20. 2 : 3

21. 1 : 6
22. 7 : 8
23. 2 : 5
24. 12 : 5

25. 1 : 3	**27.** 4 : 5	**25.** 2 : 1
26. 5 : 8	**28.** 5 : 3	**26.** 2 : 5

EXERCISE 18d
(p. 241)

1. 3 : 2	**5.** 4 : 1	**9.** 9 : 11
2. 8 : 3	**6.** 1 : 2	**10.** 5 : 2
3. 4 : 5	**7.** 2 : 3	**11.** 70 : 1
4. 5 : 1	**8.** 13 : 5	**12.** 20 : 1

13. B	**14. D**	**15. C**	**16. D**

EXERCISE 18e
(p. 242)

1. 4 : 3	**3.** 1 : 2	**5.** 3 : 8	**7.** 5 : 3
2. 5 : 3	**4.** 3 : 5	**6.** 4 : 1	**8.** 15 : 13

EXERCISE 18f
(p. 243)

1. 50 cm, 10 cm	**5.** 6 m, 8 m	**9.** 12 km, 96 km
2. 40 p, 50 p	**6.** 18 cm, 6 cm	**10.** 16, 24
3. 16 m, 56 m	**7.** 50 p, 30 p	**11.** 36 p, 30 p
4. 6 kg, 12 kg	**8.** 50 p, 70 p	

12. D	**13. D**

EXERCISE 18g
(p. 245)

1. 50 m	**2.** 100 m	**3.** 100 km	**4.** 200 m

5. 500 m	**10.** a) 9 km
6. 6 km	b) 4 km
7. 6 km	c) 6 km
8. 80 m	d) 4 km
9. 80 km	

For further practice, use any map with a simple scale.

Direct Proportion The questions in this part of the chapter can be answered by using the unitary method described, without getting involved with fractional quantities.

EXERCISE 18h
(p. 248)

1. a) 9 p	b) 90 p	**5.** a) 4 m	b) 16 m
2. a) 500 g	b) 4500 g	**6.** a) 12 p	b) 60 p
3. a) 30 p	b) £1.50	**7.** a) 70 km	b) 210 km
4. a) 4 kg	b) 20 kg		

8. 64 p	**11.** £35	**14.** £15
9. 21 minutes	**12.** 15 days	**15.** 225
10. 108 miles	**13.** £120	**16.** 2800

17. a) 5 tons	b) 210 kg	
18. a) 20	b) 400 g	c) 300 g
19. a) 150 tons	b) 20 tons	
20. a) 6 oz	b) 12 oz	c) 12

EXERCISE 18i **(p. 251)**	**1.** 5 : 1 **2.** 2 : 3 **3.** 5 : 4 **4.** 24 cm, 36 cm	**5.** 3 : 2 **6.** 100 m **7.** 10 m	

EXERCISE 18j **(p. 251)**	**1.** 1 : 4 **2.** 6 : 5 **3.** 18 : 15 **4.** 56 p : 16 p	**5.** 35 p, 45 p **6.** 35 km **7.** 200 km	

EXERCISE 18k **1.** A   **2.** B   **3.** A   **4.** D
(p. 252)

CHAPTER 19 Indices and Significant Figures

EXERCISE 19a **(p. 253)**	**1.** 8 **2.** 9	**3.** 125 **4.** 4	**5.** 16 **6.** 128

7. 6^2	**9.** 3^1	**11.** 7^4
8. 2^5	**10.** 4^2	**12.** 7^3
13. 2^8	**16.** 7^4	**19.** 5^7
14. 3^5	**17.** 3^2	**20.** 2^5
15. 5^3	**18.** 2^4	**21.** 2^1

EXERCISE 19b **(p. 254)**	**1.** 2^7 **2.** 3^5 **3.** 2^6	**4.** 2^4 **5.** 4^2 **6.** 5^4	**7.** 3^9 **8.** 2^1 **9.** 7^6	**10.** 5^5 **11.** 3^7 **12.** 3^5	**13.** 2^{10} **14.** 6^6 **15.** 6^6

Question 16 can be done with or without a scientific calculator

16. a) 128   b) 243   c) 625   d) 64
17. 3125
18. no, the base numbers are different

EXERCISE 19c $(x^2)^3$ can be worked out by multiplying the index numbers but it is not a
(p. 255) good idea to introduce the idea that indices can be multiplied when we
are emphasizing that they should be added or subtracted.

1. x^8	**4.** z^6	**7.** y^7
2. x^4	**5.** x^9	**8.** $y^6 \div x^2$
3. x^2y^6	**6.** x^3	**9.** y^8

3 and 8 cannot be simplified.

10. $6x^5$

11. $8a^8$

12. $12s^6$

13. $36y^8$

14. $20x^3$

15. $14c^7$

16. $4z^{10}$

17. $5x^5$

18. $4x^3$

19. x^8

20. y^6

21. z^9

22. x^6

23. x^8

24. y^9

25. a^{12}

26. a^{12}

27. a^8

EXERCISE 19d
(p. 257)

1. 360

2. 63 000

3. 9100

4. 26 500

5. 488

6. 54.4

7. 7 200 000

8. 478.9

9. 530 000 000

10. 380 000

11. 330

12. 152 000 000

13. 12 756

EXERCISE 19e
(p. 258)

The very large and very small numbers in these questions are unlikely to come up in other exercises but a scientific calculator produces numbers in standard form in unexpected situations and pupils need to know what to do.

1. 1.2×10^{11}

2. 1.058×10^{11}

3. 1.8×10^{15}

4. 2.061×10^{15}

5. 2.16×10^{16}

6. 1.44×10^{15}

7. 0.000 000 26

8. 0.000 001 15

9. 0.002 5

10. 0.000 15

11. 0.000 019 36

12. 0.000 016

EXERCISE 19f
(p. 260)

1. a) 2, 2 units b) 7, 7 tenths c) 5, 5 hundreds

2. a) 2, 2 hundreds b) 8, 8 tenths c) 8, 8 hundredths

3. a) 4, 4 hundreds b) 3, 3 tenths c) 3, 3 units

4. a) 4, 4 tens b) 0, no hundreds c) 3, 3 ten-thousandths

5. a) 0, no tenths b) 4, 4 thousands c) 7, 7 thousandths

6. a) 2, 2 units b) 3, 3 ten-thousandths c) 0, 0 hundred-thousandths

7. 8.3

8. 4.1

9. 2.2

10. 13

11. 170

12. 44

13. 0.82

14. 0.087

15. 0.0031

16. 9.27

17. 6.06

18. 4.40

19. 86.6

20. 759

21. 3700

22. 0.0254

23. 0.878

24. 0.000 510

25. 73

26. 0.0574

27. 889

28. 70 950

29. 0.0094

30. 3.142

31. 1.28

32. 0.7880

33. 0.002 66

EXERCISE 19g (p. 263)	**1.** $30 \times 5 = 150$; 146	**6.** $9 \times 4 = 36$; 36.5
	2. $60 \div 3 = 20$; 19.7	**7.** $300 \div 30 = 10$; 10.2
	3. $9 \times 0.2 = 1.8$; 1.76	**8.** $30 \div 5 = 6$; 5.01
	4. $600 \div 60 = 10$; 10.4	**9.** $70 \times 1 = 70$; 61.9
	5. $10 \times 25 = 250$; 343	**10.** $60 \div 2 = 30$; 33.4

11. 1620 cm^2 **13.** 466 cm   **15.** 321 000

12. 237 kg   **14.** 2.14

EXERCISE 19h
(p. 264)

1. 432   **3.** $12x^6$ **5.** 3.14 cm

2. 3^2 **4.** 47 000 (46 700)

EXERCISE 19i
(p. 264)

1. C   **3.** C   **5.** A

2. D   **4.** B   **6.** C

CHAPTER 20 Collecting Information

Pupils should by now have had some experience of collecting information. Discussion of problems already encountered will prepare them for this work.

It is also a good idea to look at some professionally prepared questionnaires and ask why they are worded the way they are.

The important points to get across are that questionnaires follow a desire to investigate specific facts or opinions. Successful questionnaires result only from clearly defined aims, and must contain clear and unambiguous questions.

Although these exercises can be done individually, the ideas do need thorough discussion afterwards.

EXERCISE 20a
(p. 266)

1. a) the bar chart with more categories has more information in it but the one with fewer categories shows the overall shape more clearly
   b) usually fewer
2. These answers are suggestions only and you may disagree with them.
   a) you would normally get enough categories by using whole number sizes only
   b) agree to take the next whole number size up for half sizes
   c) take the larger size (consistent with (b)); quite a number of people have one foot larger than the other
   d) collect the information on paper anonymously
   e) you could get idiotic answers, no answer or multiple answers; it is probably best to collect on paper but with the respondent's name attached
   f) there may be absentees from the class; pupils in another class might refuse to co-operate

Should boys and girls be considered in separate groups?

EXERCISE 20b
(p. 267)

1. Method A means that there is no way of checking who you have already asked or of checking someone's reply or of recording a reply given in an unfamiliar form that will need to be sorted out later.

2 (b) and **3** (b) e.g. absentees, embarrassment, height not known, non-cooperation

EXERCISE 20c
(p. 268)

1. This survey could be carried out in the class. The *aim* of this questionnaire should be discussed beforehand so that the results can be analysed and presented.

Questions (a) and (e) gather straightforward information but notice that the individual answers to (a) and (b) will influence the answers to (c) and (d), so that analysis is not easy.

It might be better to compose in class a questionnaire with a simpler outcome if you wish to carry out a survey. It is important for the teacher to be aware of the problems presented by a questionnaire of this type, if only to avoid them.

2. a) boys and girls grow at different rates at different ages and therefore fall into two separate groups
b) a numerical scale needs explanation

3. a) scale needs an explanation, words would be clearer
b) categories needed
c) what is meant by 'your family'; do you include yourself?

4. If parts (a) to (d) are set first then the answers can be discussed before information is collected. If this is done as a group activity each pupil need ask only a few people for the information.

CHAPTER 21 Two-way Tables and Networks

EXERCISE 21a
(p. 270)

Many other questions can be asked about these tables.

1. a) 4   b) 15   c) 22   d) 32
e) there can be no-one in that category
2. a) 1   b) 11   c) 30
3. a) 1   b) 14   c) 28
4. a) missing numbers are 4 and 9   b) 3

Other tables can be made to show information collected in the class.

EXERCISE 21b
(p. 272)

1. a) £19.20   b) £18.60   c) £35.30
d) London, Saturday + Alton towers, weekday, or Birmingham, Sunday + Alton Towers, Saturday
2. a) £49   b) £61   c) £6000, in Area 3
d) £6000, in Area 2
e) Martins £79, Barkers £68 or Martins £90, Barkers £57

3. a) 53 cm   b) size E   c) 58 cm
    d) size B; clothes can be shortened to fit but not widened
    e) size D; size C would be too small

EXERCISE 21c
(p. 275)

1. a) David   b) no, son   c) sister   d) grandfather
    e) aunt

2. a) Sally   b) older   c) we do not know
    d) and e)

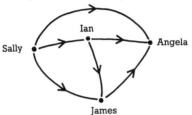

3. a) 2, 3, 4, 6   b) yes, 2   c)

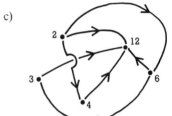

4. a) the relationship works both ways   b) yes
5. a) Philip and Martin are cousins   c)
6. b) Sarah is not a cousin of either Philip or Martin

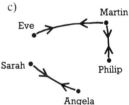

EXERCISE 21d
(p. 276)

1. a) 12 km   b) Abson, Elworth, Calbridge: 27 km; Abson, Elworth, Dacton, Calbridge: 29 km; Abson, Elworth, Dacton, Beckwith, Calbridge: 33 km; Abson, Beckwith, Calbridge 22 km; Abson, Beckwith, Dacton, Calbridge: 28 km; Abson, Beckwith, Dacton, Elsworth, Calbridge: 40 km
    c) yes   d) no
2. all are possible to draw except (b)
3. a) Through Line from A to D, then Circular Line from D to L
    b) Hook Line from I to C, then Circular Line from C to G
    c) Circular Line clockwise from N to J, then Hook Line from J to B
    Circular Line anticlockwise from N to J, then as before
    Circular Line from N (or E or D) to F, then Through Line from F (or E or D) to B
    there are other routes
5. a) yes   b) yes

6. a) Piccadilly Line; change at King's Cross onto Metropolitan Line
   b) District or Circle Line; change at Embankment onto Northern Line
   c) Northern Line; change at Elephant & Castle onto Bakerloo Line
   d) District Line; change at Gloucester Road or South Kensington onto Piccadilly Line; change at Green Park onto Jubilee Line
   e) one change (Leicester Square)
   f) no, you would have to travel right into the middle of London and out again

7. b) no   e) no
   A copymaster of a road map is given, showing the roads used in question 7 but covering a larger area. The scale of the map is twice that of published road maps so that it is easier to use. Notice that the dead ends in the copymaster are drawn open-ended (the usual convention in published road maps) while those in the pupil's book are closed.

Networks can be drawn to represent the road system round the school or home.

Maps can be obtained of the local transport system (buses, metros, trains) or of airline routes. These will present individual problems that will need thorough discussion.

CHAPTER 22 Pythagoras' Theorem ▬▬▬▬▬▬▬▬▬▬▬

EXERCISE 22a
(p. 281)

1. 16	**5.** 9	**9.** 36
2. 64	**6.** 49	**10.** 100
3. 144	**7.** 81	**11.** 400
4. 900	**8.** 1600	**12.** 4900

13. 0.09	**17.** 0.16	**21.** 0.36
14. 1.21	**18.** 1.44	**22.** 0.04
15. 0.49	**19.** 0.25	**23.** 0.0049
16. 0.0004	**20.** 0.0036	**24.** 0.000 016

25. 75.69	**29.** 53.29	**33.** 88.36
26. 18.49	**30.** 31.36	**34.** 42.25
27. 148.8	**31.** 600.3	**35.** 320.4
28. 1129	**32.** 2285	**36.** 561.7

37. 3.000	**41.** 1.999	**45.** 5.000
38. 1393	**42.** 882.7	**46.** 3163
39. 76.28	**43.** 42.95	**47.** 15.43
40. 4823	**44.** 6118	**48.** 6917

EXERCISE 22b	**1.** 4	**5.** 2	**9.** 6
(p. 282)	**2.** 9	**6.** 8	**10.** 7
	3. 1	**7.** 10	**11.** 12
	4. 3	**8.** 11	**12.** 5

13. 9.165	**16.** 4.359	**19.** 5.385
14. 12.12	**17.** 6.245	**20.** 11.75
15. 26.96	**18.** 20.78	**21.** 8.718

22. 7.893	**25.** 7.368	**28.** 2.333
23. 22.80	**26.** 6.535	**29.** 8.553
24. 1.981	**27.** 14.99	**30.** 8.591

Pythagoras' Theorem may be illustrated in the first instance by drawing squares on the sides of a 3, 4, 5 triangle. Progress from this to any right-angled triangle: measure its sides, and find the squares of these distances, to the nearest whole number, by using a calculator.

Some pupils may be interested in a variation of Pythagoras' Theorem, namely that if any mathematically similar figures are drawn on the three sides of a right-angled triangle, similar results follow, e.g.

(a)
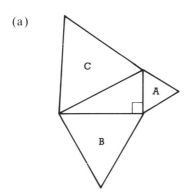

if the three equilateral triangles are drawn on the sides, then

Area C = Area A + Area B

(b)
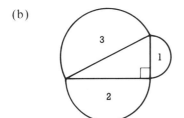

and if semicircles are drawn on the three sides, then

Area 3 = Area 1 + Area 2

EXERCISE 22c
(p. 283)

1. 29.92	**5.** 13.25	**9.** 3.972
2. 5.848	**6.** 9.182	**10.** 7.085
3. 5670	**7.** 158.8	**11.** 3329
4. 15.49	**8.** 22.36	**12.** 27.33
13. 1.322	**17.** 3.057	**21.** 5.405
14. 3.052	**18.** 87.33	**22.** 853.2
15. 6279	**19.** 357.6	**23.** 3326
16. 18.69	**20.** 27.64	**24.** 26.33

EXERCISE 22d
(p. 284)

2. $\widehat{M}$, LN	**4.** $\widehat{B}$, AC	**6.** $\widehat{C}$, AB
3. $\widehat{Q}$, PR	**5.** $\widehat{Y}$, XZ	

EXERCISE 22e
(p. 285)

These answers are calculated correct to 1 d.p.; allow an error of ±2 mm.

1. 5 cm	**4.** 8.9 cm	**7.** 1.4 cm
2. 13 cm	**5.** 10 cm	**8.** 5.8 cm
3. 6.3 cm	**6.** 7.6 cm	

9.

9	25	4	16	36	9	1	9
16	144	36	64	64	49	1	25
25	169	40	79	100	58	2	34

The third value is the sum (or very nearly) of the first two values.

EXERCISE 22f
(p. 287)

1. $AC^2 = AB^2 + BC^2$	**4.** $XZ^2 = XY^2 + YZ^2$
2. $RQ^2 = PR^2 + PQ^2$	**5.** $LN^2 = LM^2 + MN^2$
3. $BC^2 = AC^2 + AB^2$	**6.** $XY^2 = XZ^2 + YZ^2$

EXERCISE 22g
(p. 288)

1. 5 cm (exact)	**5.** 9.73 cm	**9.** 33.9 cm	**13.** 38.3 cm
2. 8.06 cm	**6.** 100 cm	**10.** 8.06 cm	**14.** 8.85 cm
3. 6.71 cm	**7.** 5.80 cm	**11.** 67.4 cm	
4. 9.43 cm	**8.** 14.9 cm	**12.** 10.2 cm	

EXERCISE 22h
(p. 291)

Pupils should be encouraged to do a complete calculation without clearing the display as this is more efficient and gives a more accurate answer. However, it is sensible to insist that intermediate calculations are written down as this acts as a check on working.

1. AB = 9.75 cm	**7.** XY = 27.7 cm
2. PQ = 28.2 cm	**8.** AB = 45.0 cm
3. LN = 19.0 cm	**9.** EF = 10.2 cm
4. XZ = 6.57 cm	**10.** PR = 16.0 cm
5. AB = 10.5 cm	**11.** AC = 53.1 cm
6. PR = 9.38 cm	**12.** QR = 3.81 cm

EXERCISE 22j   **1.** 144 yd   **3.** 122 m   **5.** 1.86 m
(p. 294)   **2.** 112 m   **4.** 31.5 m   **6.** 44.3 m

           7. 45.3 cm   **9.** 28.8 cm   **11.** 25.3 cm
           8. 32.2 cm   **10.** 22.6 cm   **12.** 14.4 cm

           13. 9.94 m   **16.** a) 4.27 m   b) 102.5 m^2
           14. 33.6 nautical miles   **17.** 2.5 m
           15. 9.30 m

EXERCISE 22k   **1.** a) 0.764   b) 35.2
(p. 297)   **2.** a) 0.296   b) 24.4
           3. 17.5 cm
           4. 3 cm
           5. 21.2 cm
           6. a) 15 cm   b) 36 cm   c) 16 cm
           7. 10 cm

CHAPTER 23   Flow Charts

Stencils to draw the 'boxes' for flow charts are available from newsagents and stationers. A copymaster at the end of this book can be used for the same purpose.

EXERCISE 23a   **1.** a) $7 + 5 = 12$ or $5 + 7 = 12$ b) $12 \div 3 = 4$ or $12 \div 4 = 3$
(p. 299)   c) $2 \times 3 - 4 = 2$ d) $3 \times 3 + 4 = 13$ or $4 + 3 \times 3 = 13$

           2. a)   b)

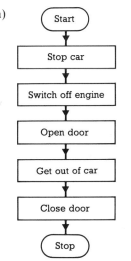

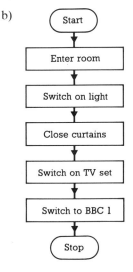

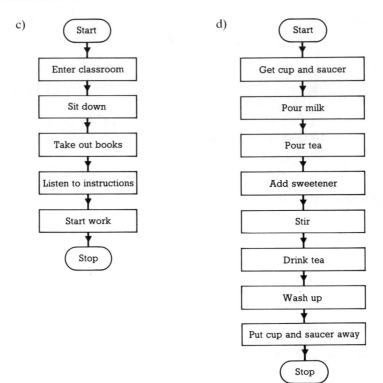

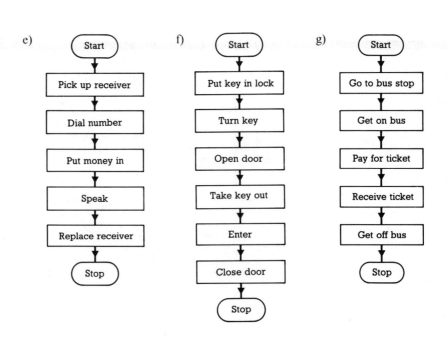

3.

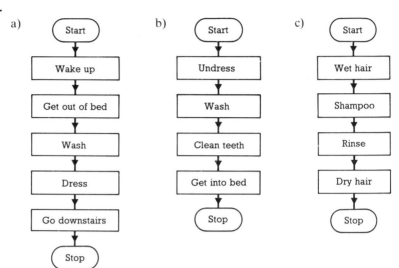

a)
- Start
- Wake up
- Get out of bed
- Wash
- Dress
- Go downstairs
- Stop

b)
- Start
- Undress
- Wash
- Clean teeth
- Get into bed
- Stop

c)
- Start
- Wet hair
- Shampoo
- Rinse
- Dry hair
- Stop

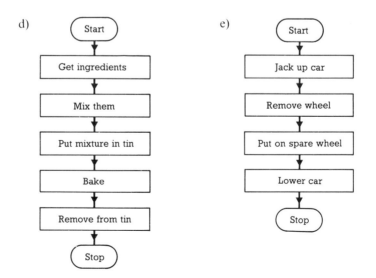

d)
- Start
- Get ingredients
- Mix them
- Put mixture in tin
- Bake
- Remove from tin
- Stop

e)
- Start
- Jack up car
- Remove wheel
- Put on spare wheel
- Lower car
- Stop

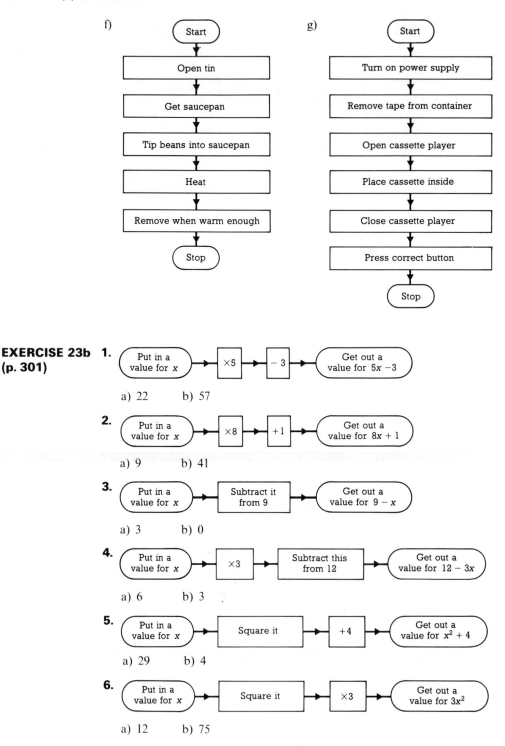

f)

Start

Open tin

Get saucepan

Tip beans into saucepan

Heat

Remove when warm enough

Stop

g)

Start

Turn on power supply

Remove tape from container

Open cassette player

Place cassette inside

Close cassette player

Press correct button

Stop

**EXERCISE 23b
(p. 301)**

1. Put in a value for x → ×5 → − 3 → Get out a value for $5x − 3$

a) 22   b) 57

2. Put in a value for x → ×8 → +1 → Get out a value for $8x + 1$

a) 9   b) 41

3. Put in a value for x → Subtract it from 9 → Get out a value for $9 − x$

a) 3   b) 0

4. Put in a value for x → ×3 → Subtract this from 12 → Get out a value for $12 − 3x$

a) 6   b) 3

5. Put in a value for x → Square it → +4 → Get out a value for $x^2 + 4$

a) 29   b) 4

6. Put in a value for x → Square it → ×3 → Get out a value for $3x^2$

a) 12   b) 75

EXERCISE 23c
(p. 302)

1.

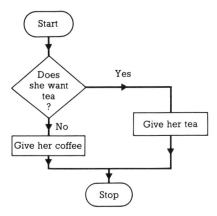

2.

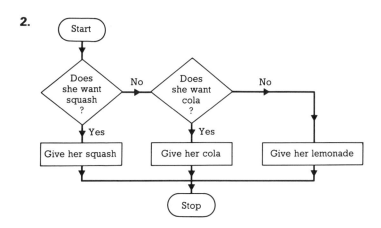

3.

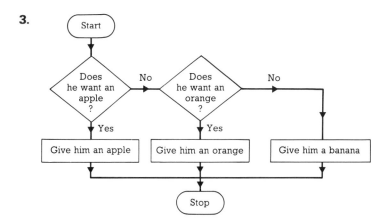

4.

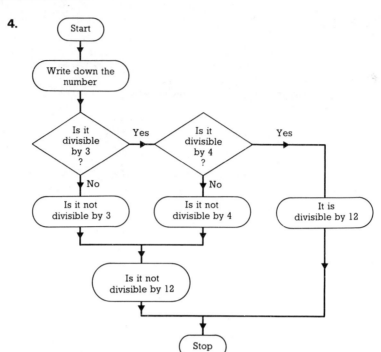

5.

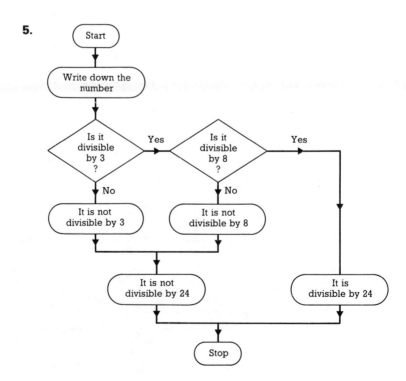

6.

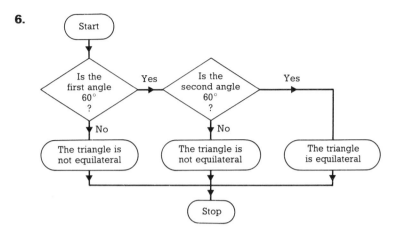

EXERCISE 23d **1.** a) to give no more than the first four terms
(p. 305)   b) 6
          c)

2. a)   7, 9, 11, 13

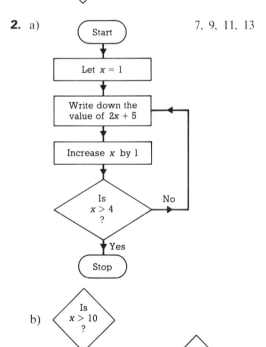

3.

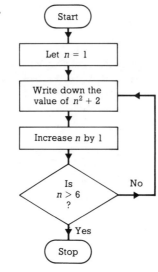

2, 6, 11, 18, 27, 38

CHAPTER 24 Coordinates and Graphs

There are two workbooks entitled *Straight Line Graphs* and *Drawing and Using Curved Graphs* which are part of the ST(P) mathematics series and which some pupils may find useful.

EXERCISE 24a
(p. 308)

This revises the use of coordinates.

1.

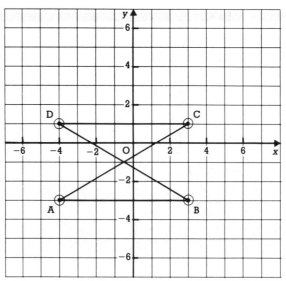

Rectangle

2.

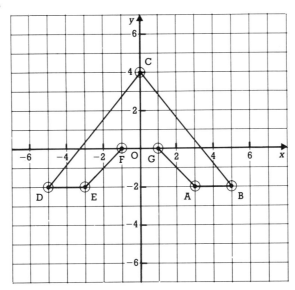

3.

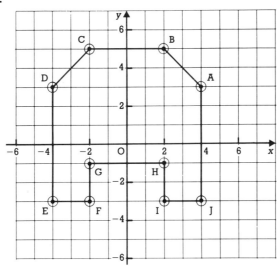

EXERCISE 24b **1.** $x = 5$ **3.** $x = -3$ **5.** $y = -2$
(p. 309)   **2.** $y = 3$ **4.** $y = 1$ **6.** $x = -4$

7.

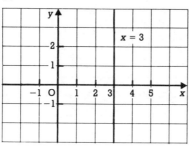

10.

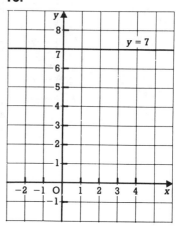

8.

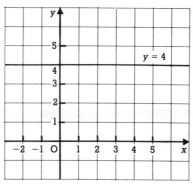

11.

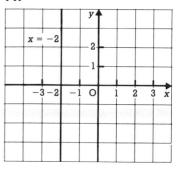

9.

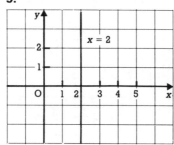

12.

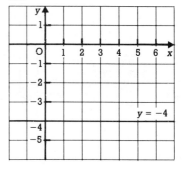

EXERCISE 24c
(p. 311)

1.

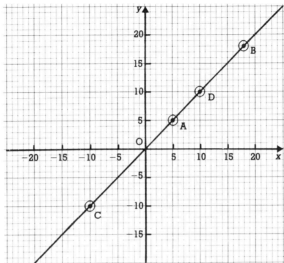

c) 10
d) they are equal
e) $y = x$

2.

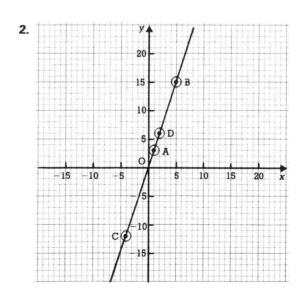

c) 6
d) y-coordinate is 3 times the x-coordinate
e) $y = 3x$

3.

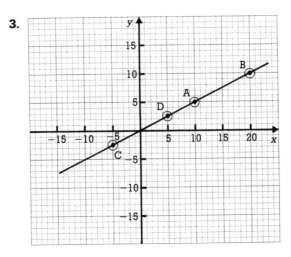

c) 2.5

d) y-coordinate is equal to half the x-coordinate

e) $y = \frac{1}{2}x$

EXERCISE 24d Using directed numbers in calculations is Level 8 work. We have included
(p. 313) it here however, because using only positive coordinates unduly restricts
the range of graphs that can be plotted; this is particularly the case with
curves.

1. −5.2	**3.** −8.5	**5.** −3.6	**7.** negative
2. −11.2	**4.** −20	**6.** −2.5	
8. −1.8	**10.** −40	**12.** −20	**14.** negative
9. −0.3	**11.** −20	**13.** −0.2	
15. 6	**17.** 9.8	**19.** 4	**21.** positive
16. 24	**18.** 0.2	**20.** 2.5	

EXERCISE 24e
(p. 315)

1. −6	**4.** 27	**7.** −12	**10.** −15
2. 12	**5.** −8	**8.** 14	**11.** 9
3. 56	**6.** 30	**9.** 4	**12.** −18
13. 2	**16.** 2	**19.** 3	**22.** −3
14. −2	**17.** −2	**20.** 5	**23.** −1
15. −2	**18.** −5	**21.** 2	**24.** −3
25. 7	**28.** 0	**31.** −3	**34.** −7
26. −1	**29.** −8	**32.** 8	**35.** −3
27. 3	**30.** 7	**33.** 19	**36.** 5
37. 6.25	**39.** −1.89		**41.** 7.5
38. 0.125	**40.** −1.31		**42.** 0.356

EXERCISE 24f   If, when the pupils plot points from their tables, the three points are not
(p. 317)   collinear, they should check all three.

1.

x	−1	0	2
y	−4	0	8

2.

x	−1	0	2
y	−6	0	12

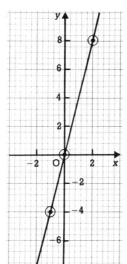

3.

x	−6	0	4
y	−3	0	2

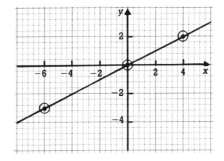

4.

x	0	2	5
y	0	−2	−5

5.

x	−2	0	4
y	4	0	−8

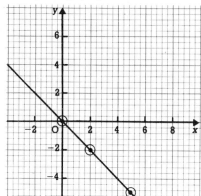

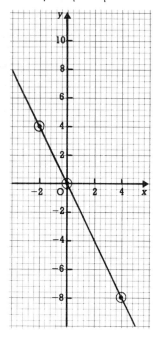

6.

x	−2	0	3
y	8	0	−12

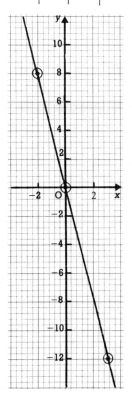

7.

x	-8	0	6
y	4	0	-3

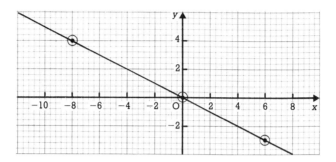

8.

x	-2	0	3
y	-6	0	9

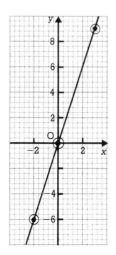

EXERCISE 24g
(p. 319)

1.

x	-1	0	2
y	-5	-3	1

2.

x	-1	0	3
y	-3	-2	1

3.

x	-2	0	2
y	-3	1	5

4.

x	-1	0	3
y	7	4	-5

5.

x	-2	0	4
y	5	3	-1

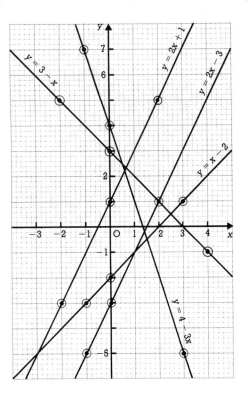

6. a) 1   b) -1 c) 0.8   d) 4   e) 2.41   f) -1.6

7. a) 2   b) -2 c) 3   d) 0   e) 0.8   f) -1.2

8. a) -2 b) 1   c) -3.4 d) -3 e) 2.6   f) -1.8

9. a)

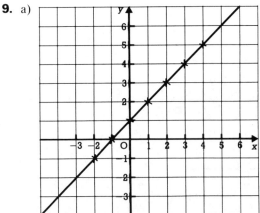

b) 8   c) 3.5   d) 31   e)

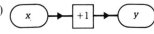

f) $y = x + 1$

10. $y = 2x + 1$

EXERCISE 24h
(p. 325)

Many pupils find drawing a smooth curve very difficult. There are various ways of improving curves: use a sharp pencil lightly so that rubbing out does not make too much mess; use several points; try to draw the curves in one pencil-stroke turning the page so that the wrist is inside the curve.

1. a)

x	-3	-2.5	-2	-1.5	-1	-0.5	0	0.5	1	1.5	2	2.5	3
y	9	6.25	4	2.25	1	0.25	0	0.25	1	2.25	4	6.25	9

c) 3.24 (± 0.1)

2. a)

x	-2	-1	-0.75	-0.5	-0.25	0	0.25	0.5	0.75	1	2
y	8	2	1.13	0.5	0.13	0	0.13	0.5	1.13	2	8

b) and c)

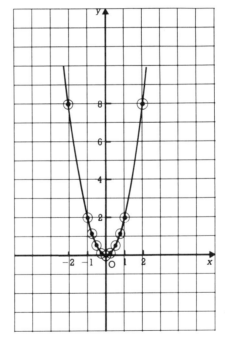

d) 4.5 (± 0.2)   e) 4.5

3. a)

x	-3	-2	-1.5	-1	-0.5	0	0.5	1	1.5	2	3
y	-7	-2	-0.25	1	1.75	2	1.75	1	-0.25	-2	-7

b) and c) see 4(b)   d) -0.56 (± 0.05)   e) the y-axis   f) 2

4. a)

x	-2	0	2
y	-5	-1	3

b)

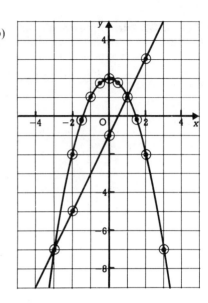

c) $(-3, -7)$, $(1, 1)$

5. a)

x	-3	-2	-1	-0.5	0	0.5	1	2	3
y	8	3	0	-0.75	-1	-0.75	0	3	8

(this is a minimum number of points)

b)

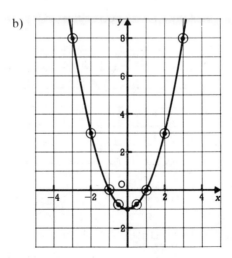

c) find y when $x = 2.5$ from the graph and from the equation; they should be the same

CHAPTER 25   Areas

EXERCISE 25a
(p. 327)
1. 5300 m
2. 28 mm
3. 170 cm
4. 520 mm
5. 5000 mm
6. 230 cm
7. 180 mm
8. 2000 mm
9. 8700 m

10. 25 cm
11. 0.5 m
12. 1 km
13. 35 cm
14. 2.5 km
15. 87.2 cm
16. 2.85 km
17. 2.8 cm
18. 0.18 km
19. 6.5 m

EXERCISE 25b
(p. 328)
1. 20 cm
2. 18 mm
3. 15 cm
4. 56 m
5. 30 cm
6. 35 cm
7. 24 cm
8. 30 cm
9. 22 cm
10. 52 cm
11. 32 cm
12. 28 cm

EXERCISE 25c
(p. 330)
1. 64 m^2
2. 12 cm^2
3. 4 mm^2
4. 32 m^2
5. 120 m^2
6. 25 cm^2
7. 160 mm^2
8. 6 cm^2
9. 6.25 m^2
10. 2.76 cm^2

11. 50 mm^2
12. 2000 cm^2
13. 15 mm^2
14. 3000 cm^2
15. 80 mm^2
16. $21\,000 \text{ cm}^2$
17. 900 mm^2
18. 660 cm^2
19. 400 mm^2
20. $12\,000 \text{ cm}^2$

EXERCISE 25d
(p. 333)
In questions such as 7, 8 and 10 pupils often have difficulty in deciding which distance to use for the height. Cardboard triangles with plumblines could well be used here.

1. 48 cm^2
2. 100 mm^2
3. 40 cm^2
4. 9 cm^2
5. 24 cm^2
6. 30 cm^2
7. 8 cm^2
8. 10 cm^2
9. 21 mm^2
10. 3 cm^2

11. 60 cm^2
12. 45 cm^2
13. 45 cm^2
14. 80 cm^2
15. 33 cm^2
16. 32.5 cm^2

EXERCISE 25e
(p. 335)
1. b) rectangle, rectangle
   c) 35 cm^2
   d) 10 cm^2
   e) 45 cm^2
2. b) rectangle, rectangle
   c) 60 cm^2
   d) 6 cm^2
   e) 66 cm^2

3. b) triangle, square
   c) 4 cm^2
   d) 16 cm^2
   e) 20 cm^2

4. b) rectangle, rectangle
   c) 18 cm^2
   d) 28 cm^2
   e) 46 cm^2

5. b) rectangle, rectangle
   c) 10 cm^2
   d) 150 cm^2
   e) 160 cm^2

6. b) triangle, triangle
   c) 24 cm^2
   d) 24 cm^2
   e) 48 cm^2

7. a) 14 cm   b) 10 cm^2
8. a) 20 cm   b) 14 cm^2

9. a) 18 cm   b) 12 cm^2
10. a) 18 cm   b) 14 cm^2

EXERCISE 25f
(p. 338)
1. 40 cm^2 **3.** 35 cm^2 **5.** 25 mm^2 **7.** 48 cm^2
2. 48 cm^2 **4.** 40 cm^2 **6.** 28 m^2 **8.** 36 cm^2

9. 63 cm^2 **10.** 48 cm^2 **11.** 80 cm^2 **12.** 81 cm^2

EXERCISE 25g
(p. 340)
1. 45 cm^2 **6.** 63 cm^2
2. 42 cm^2 **7.** 82.5 cm^2
3. 60 cm^2 **8.** 140 cm^2
4. 96 cm^2 **9.** 112 cm^2
5. 48 cm^2 **10.** 33 cm^2

EXERCISE 25h
(p. 342)
Remind pupils of the names of special quadrilaterals and their properties. To avoid the text book being marked, these questions can be copied on squared paper and duplicated.

1. a) square   c) 4 cm^2 **12.** a) rectangle   c) 4 cm^2
2. a) rectangle   c) 3 cm^2 **13.** a) trapezium   c) 7.5 cm^2
3. a) rectangle   c) 6 cm^2 **14.** a) parallelogram c) 4 cm^2
4. a) parallelogram   c) 8 cm^2 **15.** a) trapezium   c) 7 cm^2
5. a) triangle   c) 5 cm^2 **16.** a) trapezium   c) 8.5 cm^2
6. a) triangle   c) 3 cm^2 **17.** a) parallelogram c) 3.75 cm^2
7. a) triangle   c) 3 cm^2 **18.** a) rectangle   c) 7.5 cm^2
8. a) square   c) 9 cm^2 **19.** a) trapezium   c) 6 cm^2
9. a) parallelogram   c) 6 cm^2 **20.** a) parallelogram c) 10 cm^2
10. a) paralleogram   c) 4 cm^2 **21.** a) triangle   c) 6 cm^2
11. a) triangle   c) 3 cm^2 **22.** a) trapezium   c) 7.5 cm^2

EXERCISE 25i
(p. 346)
1. a) 30 000 cm^2 b) 120 000 cm^2 c) 75 000 cm^2
   d) 820 000 cm^2 e) 85 000 cm^2
2. a) 1400 mm^2 b) 300 mm^2 c) 750 mm^2
   d) 2600 mm^2 e) 3250 mm^2
3. a) 560 cm^2 b) 56 000 mm^2

4. 500 mm^2 **8.** 300 mm^2
5. 20 000 m^2 **9.** 500 000 mm^2
6. 2000 cm^2 **10.** 260 mm^2
7. 50 mm^2 **11.** 55 000 m^2

12. 3 cm^2
13. 5 ha
14. 0.25 m^2
15. 5 km
16. 27 mm

17. 0.056 m^2
18. 56.8 cm^2
19. 4.08 ha
20. 6.5 m
21. 8 ha

22. 3600 mm^2
23. 0.53 cm
24. 3.8 m
25. 980 cm

26. 2 500 000 m^2
27. 5 mm
28. 5 cm^2
29. 0.82 cm

30. a) 35 000 mm^2 b) 350 cm^2
31. a) 135 000 m^2 b) 13.5 ha
32. a) 1225 mm^2 b) 12.25 cm^2, 784 cm^2

EXERCISE 25j
(p. 347)

1. a) 80 m   b) 60 m   c) 280 m   d) 4800 m^2
2. a) 60 m   b) 18 m   c) 9 m   d) 162 m^2 e) 38 m^2 f) 54 m
3. a) 2 m   b) 5 m^2 c) 2 m^2 d) 3 m^2
4. a) 29 m   b) 8 m   c) 232 m^2 d) 300 m^2 e) 68 m^2 f) 74 m
g) 138 m
5. a) 6 m^2 b) 13 m^2 c) 7 m^2
6. a) 20 m^2 b) 2.5 m^2 c) 22.5 m^2

CHAPTER 26   Circle Calculations

It is greatly to the pupil's advantage to have a scientific calculator for this work. Anyone who does not have one will have to use 3.142 for π and may get an answer which differs slightly from the one given here.

EXERCISE 26a
(p. 350)

1. 4 mm
2. 8 cm
3. 3 cm
4. 5 cm
5. 6 mm
6. 2.4 m
7. 3 cm
8. 2 mm
9. 2.5 cm
10. 3.5 mm

EXERCISE 26b
(p. 352)

Taking 3 for the value of π gives a rough check on calculations. Using $\pi \approx 3$ is also of practical use. Pupils may well need to find a rough estimate for the distance round some circular-section object they are going to trim, bind, cover etc. Remind them that using 3 for π is an underestimate.

1. 36 cm   **3.** 24 cm   **5.** 12 mm   **7.** 60 cm   **9.** 72 m
2. 12 cm   **4.** 18 m   **6.** 48 m   **8.** 180 m   **10.** 3 m

11. 239 mm
12. 27.6 m
13. 51.5 m
14. 22.0 cm
15. 16.3 cm
16. 66.0 m
17. 79.2 cm
18. 58.4 cm
19. 1980 cm or 1.98 m

20. a) 28 cm   b) 176 cm   **25.** a) 1.75 cm   b) 11.0 cm
21. a) 4.2 cm   b) 26.4 cm   **26.** a) 3.15 cm   b) 19.8 cm
22. a) 49 cm   b) 308 cm   **27.** a) 1.05 cm   b) 6.60 cm
23. a) 7 cm   b) 44.0 cm   **28.** a) 21 cm   b) 132 cm
24. a) 1.4 cm   b) 8.80 cm

EXERCISE 26c Insist that pupils find a rough value first, by taking $\pi = 3$.
(p. 354)

1. 15.7 cm
2. 18.8 cm
3. a) 78.5 cm   b) 39.3 cm

4. a) 90 cm   b) 283 cm   c) 463 cm
5. a) each 120 cm   b) 60 cm   c) 188 cm   d) 548 cm
6. a) 30 cm   b) 94.2 cm   c) 274 cm
7. a) 1 m   b) 0.5 m   c) 1.57 m   d) 6.57 m
8. a) 30 cm   b) 94.2 cm   c) 308 cm
9. a) 40 m   b) 126 m   c) 452 m
10. a) EC = 6 cm, AD = 11 cm   b) 9.42 cm   c) 31.4 cm

EXERCISE 26d **1.** 12.6 cm^2 **4.** 113 cm^2 **7.** 6.16 cm^2 **10.** 9850 mm^2
(p. 358)   **2.** 28.3 cm^2 **5.** 3.14 cm^2 **8.** 24.6 cm^2 **11.** $12\,500 \text{ mm}^2$
                  3. 78.6 cm^2 **6.** 201 cm^2 **9.** 98.5 cm^2 **12.** 55.4 cm^2

Pupils may be intrigued to discover the increase in area caused by a
relatively small increase in radius, e.g. use a radius first of 10 cm say and
then of 12 cm. Extend the idea to other shapes; a square is an obvious
example. Taken further, the effect of enlargement on area can be
examined, but don't go into great detail concerning the exact relationships.

EXERCISE 26e **1.** 25.1 cm^2
(p. 359)   **2.** $10\,100 \text{ cm}^2$
                  3. a) 3 m   b) 14.1 m^2
                  4. 78.5 cm^2
                  5. 3.14 cm^2
                  6. a) 1600 m^2 b) 628 m^2 c) 2228 m^2
                  7. a) 1.6 m^2 b) 0.5 m   c) 0.393 m^2 d) 1.99 m^2
                  8. a) 25 cm^2 b) 19.6 cm^2 c) 44.6 cm^2
                  9. a) 314 cm^2 b) 50.3 cm^2 c) 264 cm^2
                  10. a) 240 cm^2 b) 6 cm   c) 56.6 cm^2 d) 353 cm^2

EXERCISE 26f These questions are longer and harder than any previously set in this
(p. 361)   chapter. They are not intended for weaker pupils. Taking $\pi = 3$ makes the
                  arithmetic easier, although less accurate.

1. a) 40 m^2 b) 12.6 m^2 c) 27.4 m^2 d) 12.6 m   e) 25
2. a) 65 cm   b) 1500 cm^2 c) 353 cm^2 d) 1850 cm^2 e) £11.10 f) 177 cm
3. a) 50.3 m b) 281 m   c) 20 m   d) 62.8 cm   e) 306 m f) 25 m

CHAPTER 27   Simultaneous Equations

EXERCISE 27a
(p. 363)

1. e.g. 2 and 12, 4 and 10
2. e.g. 1 and 8, 2 and 7, 3 and 6
3. e.g. 6 and 4, 8 and 6, 20 and 18
4. e.g. 4 and 8, 1 and 11   b) 12 different possibilities

5. e.g. 1, 15; 8, 8; 4, 12
6. e.g. 10, 6; 6, 2; 20, 16
7. e.g. 4, 1; 1, 7; 2, 5

8. e.g. 4, 11; 1, 8; 3, 10
9. e.g. 3, 3; 6, 2; 9, 1
10. e.g. 3, 8; 6, 6; 9, 4

11. 8
12. 12
13. 4
14. 10
15. 4
16. 3
17. 7
18. 4

EXERCISE 27b
(p. 365)

1. yes
2. no
3. no
4. yes
5. no

6. no
7. no
8. no
9. no
10. yes
11. yes

EXERCISE 27c
(p. 367)

1. $2x = 2$
2. $3p = 6$
3. $2x = 2$
4. $3a = 4$
5. $3x = 6$
6. $2x = 4$
7. $2p = 2$
8. $3a = 18$

EXERCISE 27d
(p. 368)

Checking the values of the two letters in the equation is something to be encouraged but as this can worry less able pupils do not insist too much on it.

1. $z = 2, y = 2$
2. $p = 3, q = 2$
3. $x = 2, y = 3$
4. $a = 1, b = 3$

5. $x = 1, y = 10$
6. $p = 5, q = 4$
7. $y = 2, z = 9$
8. $g = 4, h = 2$

9. You get a negative number of xs, which is not useful.
10. $x = 5, y = 1$

11. $x = 2, y = 2$
12. $z = 3, y = 2$
13. $p = 3, q = 0$
14. $x = 2, y = 5$

15. $a = 6, b = 1$
16. $q = 1, r = 11$
17. $x = 4, y = 2$
18. $a = 2, c = 15$

19. $x = 7, y = 2$
20. $p = 3, q = 4$
21. $x = 6, y = 5$

22. $a = 4, b = 4$
23. $x = 3, y = 2$
24. $x = 12, y = 1$

EXERCISE 27e
(p. 370)

1. $x = 4, y = 3$
2. $x = 7, y = 2$
3. $p = 9, q = 3$

4. $a = 1, b = 5$
5. $p = 5, q = 3$
6. $y = 1, z = 1$

7. $a = 6, b = 4$
8. $x = 4, y = 3$
9. $x = 1, y = 5$

10. $a = 4$, $b = 1$ **12.** $x = 4$, $y = 2$ **14.** $x = 3$, $y = 1$
11. $g = 3$, $h = 1$ **13.** $p = 6$, $q = 0$ **15.** $a = 10$, $c = 1$

EXERCISE 27f   **1.** $x = 2$, $y = 3$ **4.** $s = 2$, $t = 4$ **7.** $a = 3$, $b = 8$
(p. 371)   **2.** $x = 1$, $y = 1$ **5.** $p = 0$, $q = 6$ **8.** $a = 0$, $c = 18$
                   3. $h = 5$, $k = 1$ **6.** $p = 1$, $q = 2$ **9.** $a = 4$, $c = 1$

10. $x = 5$, $y = 2$ **13.** $p = 1$, $q = 7$ **16.** $a = 2$, $c = 5$
11. $x = 1$, $y = 2$ **14.** $p = 1$, $q = 6$ **17.** $g = 6$, $h = 2$
12. $x = 2$, $y = 5$ **15.** $p = 1$, $q = 1$ **18.** $y = 5$, $z = 8$

19. a) $x = 25$, $y = 10$ b) adult's fare is 25 p, child's fare is 10 p
20. a) $x = 28$, $y = 12$ b) 28 large boxes, 12 small ones

EXERCISE 27g   **1.** 4   **4.** e.g. 1, 10; 2, 6; 3, 3
(p. 372)   **2.** no   **5.** $x = 2$, $y = 3$
                   3. $p = 7$, $q = 1$

EXERCISE 27h   **1.** 4   **4.** $p = 7$, $q = 5$
(p. 373)   **2.** e.g. 6, 4; 5, 2; 4, 0   **5.** 4
                   3. $x = 7$, $y = 4$

CHAPTER 28   Using Negative Numbers in Equations and Formulae ▬

This chapter gives practice in calculating with negative numbers in a different context from Chapter 24. It is optional.

EXERCISE 28a   **1.** 5   **3.** 25   **5.** -20 **7.** 9
(p. 374)   **2.** -2 **4.** -5 **6.** 5   **8.** 3

EXERCISE 28b   **1.** -6 **4.** -6 **7.** -16 **10.** -9
(p. 374)   **2.** -10 **5.** 7   **8.** 5   **11.** -14
                   3. -3 **6.** -12 **9.** 10   **12.** 3.5

EXERCISE 28c   **1.** -3 **4.** -8 **7.** -1
(p. 375)   **2.** -1 **5.** -1 **8.** -2
                   3. -4 **6.** -3 **9.** -5

10. -2 **13.** -2 **16.** -1
11. -8 **14.** -2 **17.** -6
12. -2 **15.** -1 **18.** -4

19. $x = -2$, $-2°C$ **20.** $x = -2$, basement

EXERCISE 28d **(p. 377)**	**1.** 6	**2.** -7	**3.** -3	**4.** 7	**5.** 9
	6. -3	**7.** -9	**8.** -5	**9.** -8	**10.** 2
	11. -4		**12.** -2		**13.** -2

EXERCISE 28e **(p. 378)**	**1.** -6	**4.** a) 19	b) 6	c) -1
	2. -2	**5.** a) -5.5	b) 8	
	3. -15	**6.** a) 77	b) 5	c) $23\,°F$

EXERCISE 28f **(p. 379)**	**1.** B	**3.** C	**5.** C
	2. B	**4.** B	**6.** A

CHAPTER 29   Revision Exercises

EXERCISE 1 **(p. 380)**	**1.** B	**4.** D	**7.** C	**10.** B	**13.** B
	2. C	**5.** C	**8.** B	**11.** B	**14.** C
	3. A	**6.** A	**9.** C	**12.** C	**15.** B

EXERCISE 2 **(p. 382)**	**1.** B	**4.** D	**7.** B	**10.** A
	2. C	**5.** A	**8.** C	**11.** B
	3. D	**6.** D	**9.** A	**12.** D

EXERCISE 3 **(p. 385)**	**1.** D	**4.** A	**7.** B	**10.** D
	2. A	**5.** C	**8.** D	**11.** B
	3. C	**6.** B	**9.** B	**12.** A

MENTAL TESTS

TEST 1
1. Write down, in figures, the number four thousand and fifty two. — 4052
2. Write down the prime numbers that are less than 10. — 2, 3, 5, 7
3. Is the number 1731 divisible by 3? — yes
4. Write down the prime factors of 14. — 2, 7
5. What are the multiples of 3 between 10 and 20? — 12, 15, 18
6. Find $2 \times 3 \times 2$ — 12
7. What is the value of 2 cubed? — 8
8. Find $13 + 2 + 8$ — 23
9. Calculate $2 - 4$ — -2
10. Find 20×300 — 6000

TEST 2
1. Write down all the factors of 6. — 1, 2, 3, 6
2. Find $2500 \div 50$ — 50
3. What is the remainder when 16 is divided by 3? — 1
4. What is the lowest number that is a multiple of both 4 and 6? — 24
5. What is the highest number that is a factor of both 4 and 6? — 2
6. Find $10 \times 4 \times 7$ — 280
7. Find the value of 2 to the power 4 — 16
8. What is the remainder when 54 is divided by 7? — 5
9. Find 20×120 — 2400
10. Find $-2 + 9$ — 7

TEST 3
1. Find one fifth of £50. — £10
2. Write down, in figures, the number seventy thousand, one hundred and five. — 70 105
3. Simplify $\frac{3}{9}$ as far as possible. — $\frac{1}{3}$
4. Find $3 \times 2 \times 4$ — 24
5. Express two fifths as tenths. — $\frac{4}{10}$
6. Find $\frac{7}{12} - \frac{1}{12}$ — $\frac{1}{2}$
7. Find the value of 9 squared. — 81
8. Change $\frac{8}{3}$ into a mixed number. — $2\frac{1}{3}$
9. Write down the prime factors of 18. — 2, 3
10. Express $2\frac{3}{4}$ as an improper fraction. — $\frac{11}{4}$

TEST 4
1. Which is smaller, 1.5 or 1.05? — 1.05
2. Write 1 and $\frac{3}{10}$ as a decimal. — 1.3
3. Write down the figure in the second decimal place in 1.243 — 4

4. Write 0.75 as a fraction. $\frac{3}{4}$

5. What is the lowest number that is a multiple of both
4 and 5? 20

6. What is the remainder when 32 is divided by 5? 2

7. Express $\frac{7}{100}$ as a decimal. 0.07

8. Find 3600 ÷ 300 12

9. Find 2.3 + 0.2 2.5

10. Express 0.8 as a fraction in its lowest terms. $\frac{4}{5}$

TEST 5

1. Express 0.05 as a fraction in its lowest terms. $\frac{1}{20}$

2. Find 4 × 3 × 5 60

3. Write $2\frac{3}{4}$ as a decimal. 2.75

4. Find 12.6 ÷ 10 1.26

5. Give 0.0159 correct to 3 decimal places. 0.016

6. Write $\frac{26}{5}$ as a mixed number. $5\frac{1}{5}$

7. Find 2.5 − 0.3 2.2

8. What are the factors of 8? 1, 2, 4, 8

9. Find 6.03 × 100 603

10. Express $\frac{1}{3}$ as a decimal correct to 2 decimal places. 0.33

TEST 6

1. Write $3x + x$ in as simple a form as possible. $4x$

2. Find $\frac{2}{5}$ of £5.20. £2.08

3. Find 30 × 1200 36 000

4. Write "a multiplied by a" in as simple a form as possible. a^2

5. Find 2745 ÷ 1000 2.745

6. Simplify $2x \times 3x$ $6x^2$

7. The sizes of two of the angles in a triangle are 30° and 60°.
What is the size of the other angle? 90°

8. Find $\frac{1}{5}$ of 43 p correct to the nearest penny. 9 p

9. Write down the next two numbers in this sequence:
4, 9, 16 25, 36

10. In an isosceles triangle, how many of the sides are
the same length? 2

TEST 7

1. Find 40 × 50 2000

2. Write down all the factors of 20 1, 2, 4, 5, 10, 20

3. What is the square of 5? 25

4. Give the next number in the number pattern 4, 7, 10 ... 13

5. Express one quarter as a percentage. 25%

6. Is the number 135 divisible by 5? yes

7. Calculate 6 − 10 −4

8. What is the remainder when 36 is divided by 7? 1

9. What do the angles round a point add up to? 360°

10. What is 100% of £6? £6

TEST 8

1. Find $7000 \div 100$ 70
2. Find 50% of £18.   £9
3. What is the square root of 36?   6
4. Find 7.2×10 72
5. What is the size of an angle of an equilateral triangle?   60°
6. Find $70 \div 100$ 0.7
7. Express 70% as a fraction, as simply as possible. $\frac{7}{10}$
8. If $y = 4$, what is the value of $y + 3$?   7
9. If I throw a dice, what is the probability that I get 6? $\frac{1}{6}$
10. Find $32 + 29$ 61

TEST 9

1. Find 15×3 45
2. Find $3 - 7$ -4
3. What percentage is 8 cm of 16 cm?   50%
4. If I toss a coin 200 times, roughly how many heads would I expect to get?   100
5. In a class, 55% are boys. What percentage are girls?   45%
6. Find 20×20 400
7. How many faces has a cube?   6
8. Simplify $6z - 2z$ $4z$
9. Find $64 \div 2$ 32
10. Write down the prime factors of 15.   3, 5

TEST 10

1. Find $62 \div 10$ 6.2
2. Express three quarters as a percentage.   75%
3. If I toss an unbiased coin, what is the probability that I get a head? $\frac{1}{2}$
4. What is the name of a quadrilateral with four equal sides and four right angles?   square
5. Is 16 a multiple of 3?   no
6. Find 25% of 20 km.   5 km
7. How far does Mr Baker travel if he drives for 2 hours at 50 mph?   100 miles
8. What is the value of $4c$ if $c = 3$?   12
9. Which unit would you use to measure a quantity of paint, litres or square metres?   litres
10. Find $7 - 9 + 2$ 0

TEST 11

1. Express $\frac{3}{100}$ as a decimal.   0.03
2. At what steady speed am I walking if I walk 6 miles in 2 hours?   3 mph
3. Take 10 from 7. -3
4. What percentage is £2 of £8?   25%
5. Give the square root of 49.   7
6. Write as simply as possible, x multiplied by x multiplied by x x^3
7. Give $\frac{11}{7}$ as a mixed number. $1\frac{4}{7}$

8.	Find 3 cubed.	27
9.	Find $6000 \div 20$	300
10.	Express 17% as a fraction.	$\frac{17}{100}$

TEST 12

1.	In a car park, 15% of the cars are white. What percentage are not white?	85%
2.	Express 0.3 as a fraction.	$\frac{3}{10}$
3.	What do the angles of a quadrilateral add up to?	360°
4.	Write as simply as possible, $2x + 3x$	$5x$
5.	Find $8 + 7 + 9$	24
6.	Find one third of 21 km	7 km
7.	Write down, in figures, the number twenty thousand and two.	20 002
8.	Give 2.432 correct to 2 decimal places.	2.43
9.	Give 2.432 correct to 2 significant figures.	2.4
10.	Give the next number in the number pattern 1, 2, 4, 8,...	16

TEST 13

1.	Express $\frac{7}{10}$ as a decimal.	0.7
2.	Write down the square root of 121.	11
3.	Simplify $5a - 9a$	$-4a$
4.	How far does Sonia travel if she cycles for 2 hours at 15 km/h?	30 km
5.	What is the smallest number that is exactly divisible by both 3 and 5?	15
6.	Change $\frac{11}{4}$ into a mixed number.	$2\frac{3}{4}$
7.	Tim spins a 5 p coin 500 times. Roughly how many heads does he expect to get?	250
8.	What direction is opposite to east?	west
9.	Is it true that -4 is smaller than -5?	no
10.	Find the value of 2^4?	16

TEST 14

1.	Express 0.75 as a fraction in its lowest terms.	$\frac{3}{4}$
2.	Find $3.2 + 1.5$	4.7
3.	Simplify $\frac{15}{21}$ as far as possible.	$\frac{3}{7}$
4.	What is the value of 3 to the power 3?	27
5.	Would you measure the area of a room in cubic metres or in square metres?	square metres
6.	What percentage is 6 m of 12 m?	50%
7.	What do the angles on a straight line add up to?	180°
8.	Simplify the ratio 10 : 15.	2 : 3
9.	Write 3×10^2 as an ordinary number.	300
10.	Write down the second significant figure in 2457.	4

TEST 15

1.	Express $\frac{19}{100}$ as a decimal.	0.19
2.	Simplify $6a + 8a$	$14a$

3. In a box of oranges 5% are bad.
What percentage are good?   95%
4. Find 75% of 40 km.   30 km
5. In a class, 80% of the pupils have done their homework.
What percentage have not?   20%
6. How many corners does a cube have?   8
7. If six envelopes cost 48 p how much will two cost?   16 p
8. Multiply 2.3 by 10^3.   2300
9. How many degrees are there in one quarter of a
revolution?   90°
10. Express 3 litres in cubic centimetres.   3000 cm^3

TEST 16

1. Give the square root of 64.   8
2. Express one and four-fifths as an improper fraction. $\frac{9}{5}$
3. Find 3.5 − 1.7   1.8
4. What is remainder when 19 is divided by 4?   3
5. Is 34 exactly divisible by 4?   no
6. Would you measure your height in kilometres or in
centimetres?   cm
7. Divide 12 cm into two parts in the ratio 1 : 2.   4 cm, 8 cm
8. Is it true that −3 is greater than −5?   yes
9. Which direction is opposite to south?   north
10. Two angles in a triangle are each 70°.
What is the size of the third angle?   40°

TEST 17

1. What is the probability that Sally scores an even number
when she throws a dice? $\frac{1}{2}$
2. Write down, in figures, the number
fifteen hundred and three   1503
3. Find the value of 5a when a is 3.   15
4. How far can Don expect to go on 5 litres of petrol if his
car goes 12 km on 1 litre of petrol.   60 km
5. Write as simply as possible,
a multiplied by itself four times. a^4
6. Find 8 − 12 + 5   1
7. Write down the next two prime numbers after 11.   13, 17
8. If b = 5 what is the value of 2b − 10?   0
9. Express $\frac{2}{3}$ as a decimal correct to 2 decimal places.   0.67
10. Name the object that Nazim is looking at if the plan,
front elevation and side elevation are all squares.   cube

TEST 18

1. Write down, in figures, the number
three thousand and sixteen.   3016
2. Express 5 cm as a percentage of 20 cm.   25%
3. Find Alf's average speed, if he walks 12 miles in 3 hours.   4 mph
4. Write down the next number in the sequence
1, 3, 9, 27, . . .   81

5.	Find $\frac{3}{4}$ of 24 litres.	18
6.	Give, correct to 2 significant figures, the number fifty four thousand three hundred and twenty one.	54 000
7.	Divide 20 g into two parts in the ratio 3 : 2.	12 g, 8 g
8.	Find $\frac{4}{5}$ of 40 m.	32 m
9.	Express $\frac{3}{4}$ in twelfths.	$\frac{9}{12}$
10.	What is the largest number that is a factor of both 18 and 27?	9

TEST 19

1.	What is the square root of 81?	9
2.	Give due east as a three-figure bearing.	090°
3.	What is the remainder when 31 is divided by 7?	3
4.	Divide £20 in the ratio 3 : 1.	£15, £5
5.	What percentage of 10 weeks is 2 weeks?	20%
6.	What number is 2 greater than -5?	-3
7.	What is the third angle of a triangle if two of the angles are 60° and 40°?	80°
8.	Give $\frac{7}{50}$ as a percentage.	14%
9.	Which number is greater, fourteen hundred and two or one thousand four hundred?	1402
10.	Which direction is opposite to NW?	SE

TEST 20

1.	Express $\frac{2}{3}$ in ninths.	$\frac{6}{9}$
2.	What is the largest number that is a factor of both 15 and 24?	3
3.	Is 11 the square root of 132?	no
4.	Give, correct to two significant figures, the number 357.	360
5.	What percentage of a class are girls if 45% of the pupils in the class are boys?	55%
6.	A rectangle measures 8 cm by 7 cm. What is its area?	56 cm^2
7.	Which is greater, -7 or -4?	-4
8.	Give, correct to one decimal place, the number 5.05.	5.1
9.	Give the smallest number that is a multiple of both 8 and 6.	24
10.	What is 10% of 40 hours?	4 hours

TEST 21

1.	Give $\frac{37}{9}$ as a mixed number.	$4\frac{1}{9}$
2.	What is the value of $4x$ if $x = -3$	-12
3.	What is the radius of a circle with diameter 14 cm?	7 cm
4.	Is the square root of 400 equal to 20 or 200?	20
5.	What is the area of a triangle with base 10 cm and height 8 cm?	40 cm^2
6.	Which is greater -9 or 1?	1
7.	What percentage of 50 is 40?	80
8.	Is 456 a multiple of 3?	yes
9.	What three-figure bearing represents due west?	270°
10.	What is $\frac{1}{3}$ of 27?	9

TEST 22

1. What is the remainder when 45 is divided by 7?   3
2. Find a rough value for the circumference of a circle with diameter 4 cm.   12 cm
3. What is the largest number that is a factor of both 12 and 28?   4
4. Which compass direction has a bearing of 180°?   south
5. Express $\frac{1}{10}$ as a percentage.   10%
6. Would you measure the volume of a room in square metres or cubic metres?   cubic metres
7. Simplify $3x - 8x$ $-5x$
8. Give, correct to two significant figures, the number 876.   880
9. Rick takes a coin from his pocket. What is the probability that it is a £1 coin if there are three £1 coins and four 5 p coins in that pocket? $\frac{3}{7}$
10. In a triangle, two of the angles are each 50°. What is the size of the third angle?   80°

TEST 23

1. Winston takes a sweet from a packet containing 3 toffees and 5 chocolates. What is the probability that it will be a toffee? $\frac{3}{8}$
2. Find the value of $6a$ when a is -5. -30
3. What is the largest number that is a factor of both 27 and 45?   9
4. Give the value of 5 cubed.   125
5. What is Raj's average speed if he cycles 48 km in 4 hours?   12 km/h
6. Is -11 greater than -4?   no
7. What, roughly, is the area of a circle with radius 2 cm?   12 cm^2
8. What percentage of £10 is £7?   70%
9. Give, correct to one significant figure, the number 55.   60
10. Which compass direction has a three-figure bearing of 270°?   west

TEST 24

1. What is the volume of a cube of side 3 cm?   27 cm^3
2. What is the remainder when 51 is divided by 8?   3
3. What is the smallest number that is a multiple of both 8 and 20?   40
4. Give a rough value for the circumference of a circle with diameter 6 cm.   18 cm
5. What is 40% of £10?   £4
6. Would you measure the area of a circle in centimetres or square centimetres?   cm^2
7. Express 20% as a fraction in its simplest terms. $\frac{1}{5}$
8. Is 36 exactly divisible by 8?   no
9. If seven ballpens cost 84 p, what does one cost?   12 p
10. Give, to the nearest thousand, the number seventeen hundred and eighty.   2000

COPYMASTER 1

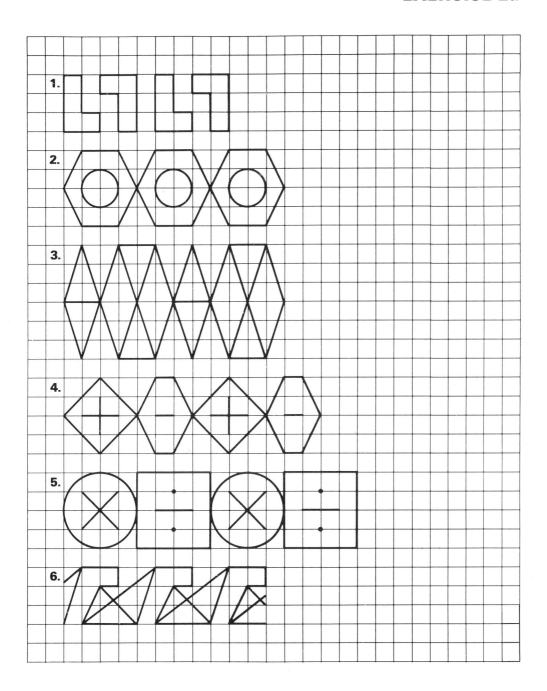

COPYMASTER 2

CHAPTER 11

Complete the following plans and elevations.

1.

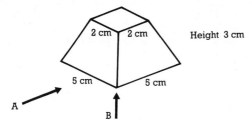

2 cm 2 cm   Height 3 cm

5 cm   5 cm

A

B

Plan   Elevation from A   Elevation from B

2.

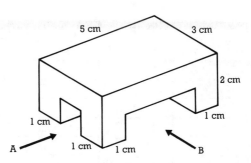

5 cm   3 cm

2 cm

1 cm   1 cm

A   1 cm   1 cm   B

Plan   Elevation from A   Elevation from B

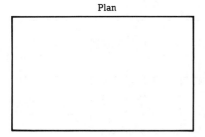

COPYMASTER 3

EXERCISE 15d

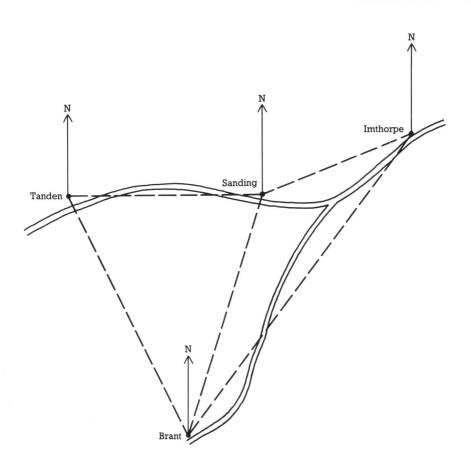

COPYMASTER 4

EXERCISE 15e

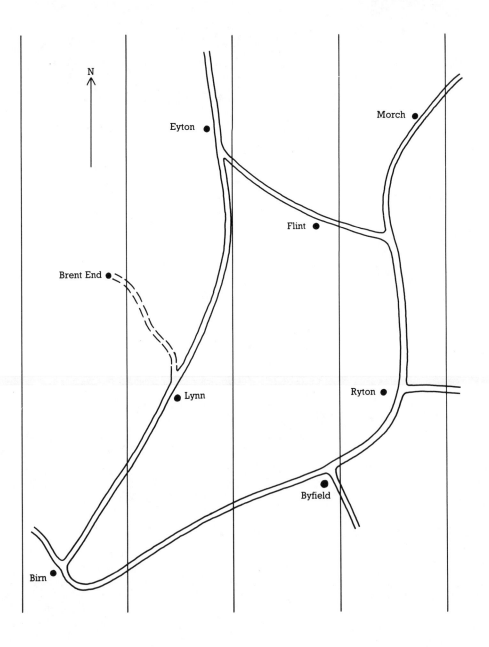

COPYMASTER 5

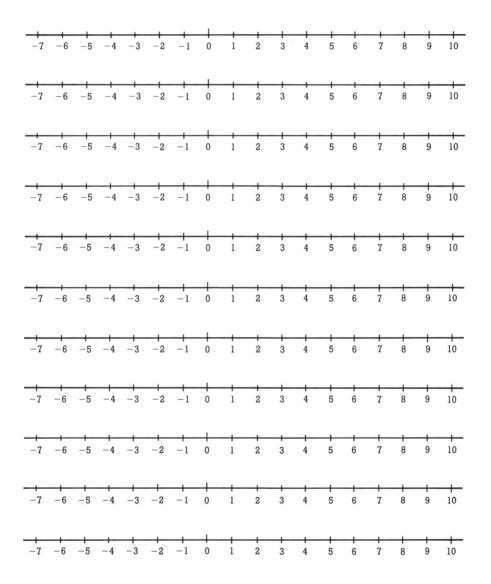

COPYMASTER 6

EXERCISE 21d, Q. 7

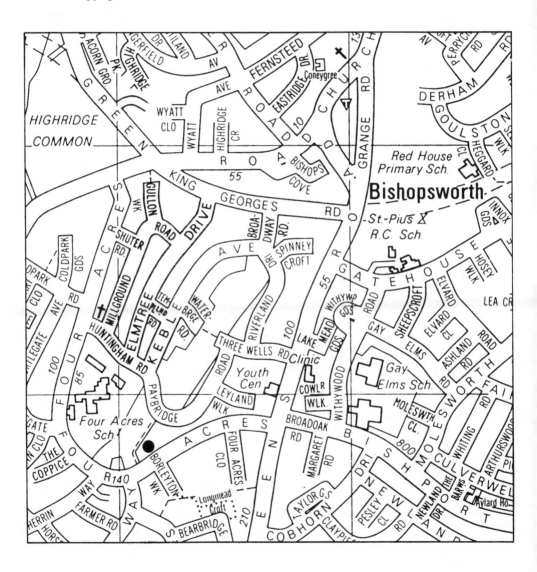

COPYMASTER 7

CHAPTER 13

State whether each quadrilateral is a square, a rectangle, a parallelogram, a rhombus, a trapezium, a kite or none of these.

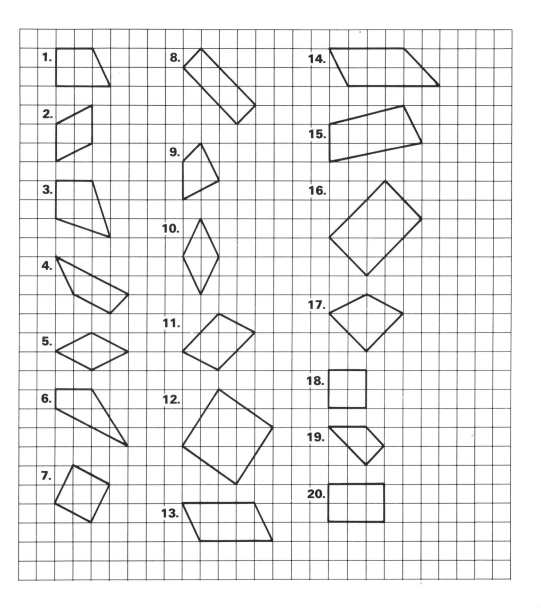

COPYMASTER 8

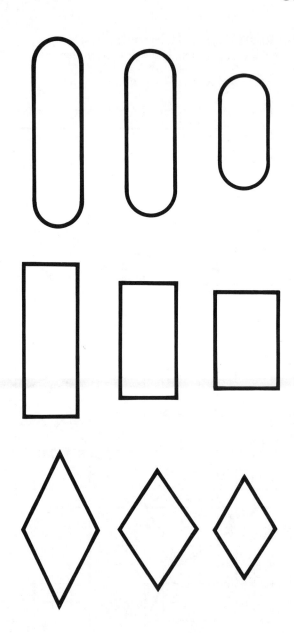